Praise for

A Common Thread

There is no one I believe in more than Jen Principe when it comes to making you feel your best. Jen came into my life at a very difficult time and because of her passion, talent, vision, and style, I regained my confidence and felt beautiful for the first time in a long time. Jen's memoir is a perfect reflection of her: it's empowering, brave, and sincere. This emotional memoir weaves faith and fashion together in a whole new light.

—**Ellen Rakieten,** Executive Producer/Writer
for *Red Table Talk* and *The Oprah Winfrey Show*

A Common Thread is a poignant, honest, and inspiring book that cleverly weaves in the psychological impact that clothes can have on personal transformation.

—**Dr. Jenn Mann,** Author of *The Relationship Fix:
Dr. Jenn's 6-Step Guide to Improving Communication, Connection & Intimacy,*
Host of VH1 *Couples Therapy*

A Common Thread is a fresh, fun, and honest look at how fashion and life are directly intertwined. Viewing fashion through the lens of Jen Principe, you'll see your wardrobe in a whole new light. This heartfelt and spunky book will encourage you to take a look at your relationship with style and, through Jen's story, will guide you toward an unexpected and exciting journey to craft your own fashion story.

—**Courtney Sixx,** How2Girl, Founder of Bouquet Box

Jen Principe intertwines stories of resilience, faith, and healing and reminds us that anyone's life can be transformed. This is more than just a fashion book.

—**Gaby Symon,** Host of SiriusXM Hits 1

Jen Principe's advice is life-changing! *A Common Thread* is a poignant, inspirational memoir that has inspired me to step out of my comfort zone and look at my career, wardrobe, and life from an entirely new perspective and rise to the next level of success all around.

—Dr. Tanya Altmann, Pediatrician, Mom, Author,
Media Spokesperson, On-camera Medical Correspondent

a common thread

© 2022 Jen Principe
A Common Thread: A Fashion for the Soul Book

First edition, June 2022

Published by Jen Principe
Thousand Oaks, CA

www.jpstyles.com

Editing: Audrey Yap
Proofreading: Shayla Raquel, shaylaraquel.com
Cover Design & Illustrations: Elizabeth Turner Stokes
Photographer: Images of Life by Ashli Photography, imagesoflifebyashli.com
Interior Formatting: Melinda Martin, melindamartin.me

This is a work of creative nonfiction. The events are portrayed to the best of Jen Principe's memory. While all the stories in this book are true, some names and identifying details have been changed to protect the privacy of the people involved.

ISBN: 979-8-9860664-0-0 (hardcover), 979-8-9860664-1-7 (paperback)

a common thread

A FASHION FOR THE SOUL BOOK

JEN PRINCIPE

This book is dedicated to my father,
who did the best he could
and left this earth too soon.

HOW IT WORKS

Contents

INTRODUCTION

I was once featured as a celebrity fashion stylist on a UK show called *Inside Beverly Hills*, which aired on the nation's largest network (BBC). The show highlighted the world's most glamorous and iconic places, and the episode I was on was all about style, status, and spending—things I am very well versed in. It was an honor to be chosen as the show's only fashion stylist, as someone who dresses some of the wealthiest business professionals and celebrities in the world.

As we were winding down on the third day of taping, the producer and I began sharing some personal stories from our upbringing. After learning about just a snippet of my past, the producer looked at me and said, "Wait, you mean you weren't born in a Fabergé egg?"

I laughed. I had heard similar comments in my years, but I had never heard *that one* before. No, I was not born in a Fabergé egg. Far from it, actually. But I understand how one might think that, especially looking at my life today. I live in a traditional East Coast–style two-story home in a gated, upscale community. I have two successful sons and a handsome, doting husband. I have gorgeous friends and a thriving, successful career. I'm surrounded by the most coveted and luxurious fashions and the rarest, most exotic cars in the world, and I attend extravagant, exclusive parties. I enjoy traveling first class and, of course, I have a closet filled with fabulous clothes. I don't *have* to work; I *choose* to work. And because of these things, coupled with the fact that I can be a little guarded, I'm frequently misunderstood or, rather, prejudged.

I'm used to it. I have been judged my entire life. As a child, growing up in a small religious community, I was quickly labeled a "problem child" and not to be played with because I was from a broken home. As a teenager, I was

1

labeled a "juvenile delinquent." And, today, I've been labeled an "entitled rich housewife."

If there are two axioms that ring true, it's that we don't know what goes on behind closed doors and rarely do we know what someone has been through. Our childhoods, even the apparently happy ones, have an impact on the lens through which we see the world and behave. We are all just products of our past, and mine has certainly shaped my emotional wounds and the trajectory of my life. While it might appear that my life is perfect, I assure you that it *isn't*. There's no such thing.

Abandonment and abuse have lived as my primary wounds for decades, reinforcing beliefs that I was fundamentally broken and not good enough. My family climate was, needless to say, traumatic. Many have remarked that it's miraculous I've ended up so "normal," which has always made me chuckle. I don't think I'm normal, and I haven't "ended up" anywhere yet. I'm a work in progress.

My past has included its fair share of drinking, smoking, stealing, drugs, arrests, avoiding my feelings, sweeping things under the rug to avoid conflict, underachieving, overachieving, depression, and low self-esteem. My pistanthrophobia (fear of trusting people) is still alive and well.

But if you want to know what I think has saved my life, it's the "F" words. I have been using them since as far back as I can remember. The first time I remember becoming uncontrollably angry and using an "F" word, I was ten years old. My face swollen and still stinging from the slaps across my cheeks, my arms bright red from being pinched, I ran to my room, slammed my door shut, fell to my knees, and used it. It immediately calmed me, and after that experience, I began using it all the time. It became a form of meditation for me and helped to soothe my pain. And, no, it's not the word you're thinking about! While using profanity sometimes feels good and has helped me cope with situations where I felt I had no control, I'm referring to a different "F" word: *faith*. When practiced with prayer, faith is a powerful action word that I have used throughout my life.

The other "F" word that I'm referring to is "fashion," clothing in particular. It has played many different roles in my life. It's been a gift of both talent and teaching. Fashion has served as a healing modality, but it has also been a curse, landing me in jail several times. (But more on this later.) It has forced me to face some of my demons and make an honest appraisal of myself and my attachments to my image and material things. Fashion has helped me see and accept my role as a stylist, ultimately finding my purpose in helping others transform from the outside in.

Rarely do we know our own unique design as it's being stitched together until we are able to recognize a *common thread*. Faith and fashion have been the two constants in my life, intertwined for as long as I can remember, both weaving a pattern throughout my life and planting the seeds for my adult self.

I grew up in a religious home. My grandfather was the chief Orthodox rabbi of Los Angeles from 1935 to 1973. He was one of the most prominent and powerful figures in the Orthodox Jewish community and pioneered the first Hebrew parochial day school in Los Angeles. Right out of preschool, I attended Emek Hebrew Academy in North Hollywood.

And while I spent years at such schools to study my religion and learn about its culture, belief systems, laws, and tradition, it has been *clothing* that has taught me some of my most valuable lessons and the basic virtues of life.

I have been in and out of closets curating looks from walking the red carpet to running to the grocery store. I am a personal fashion stylist whose client list has run the gamut: celebrities, musicians, producers, directors, doctors, attorneys, business moguls, and even stay-at-home moms. I have learned that no matter where you are on the ladder or what profession you hold, no matter your economic status, race, or religion, changing your wardrobe can change your *energy*—and for the better. My clients feel more confident and self-assured, and they experience more overall joy in their lives. But I knew this well before I entered the fashion world.

Clothes have been a part of my life since as far back as I can remember. I've always known intrinsically that you could "change" your look and "become" or feel like someone else. As a child, I did this often because I wanted to be anyone but me. Playing dress-up was more than just about being a fairy-tale princess; it was my escape. Growing up in an abusive and alcoholic home, I used clothing to hide, protect, escape, support, and define myself as a child and into my late teenage years. But at some point, I couldn't hide behind a coat of armor. Eventually, I had to probe the depths and heal the cracks.

Through a series of unrelated and seemingly inconsequential occurrences (at the time, at least), I began to see a pattern. God was speaking to me in the one language I understood: clothing. No path is linear, and mine has pivoted in many different directions, but as I continued to listen to my inner voice, it ultimately led me here, to writing this book. On my journey, I have learned that, paradoxically, there is space in the spiritual realm for the material world too. I have seen the transformations with my clientele and have gained some very profound wardrobe wisdom.

As I began diving deeper into these serendipitous encounters in my life, I learned about acceptance, forgiveness, humility, expectations, letting go of attachments, and being of service—all in the most unexpected ways. And each story involves faith or fashion. From saving a man who considered jumping off a bridge, to sending a Holocaust survivor across the globe to meet his only surviving relative, to meeting a monk who propelled me forward into writing this book, to reclaiming my mojo from a most unexpected source, to ultimately finding my purpose in helping others rise from the ashes, like phoenixes birthed anew.

In this book, you will learn about the meaning and the messages that lie behind the clothes we wear and how they can affect our lives, from the boardroom to the bedroom and everything in between. In it, you will also get the practical applications with the latest innovative QR-code technology, which will lead you to tutorials on how to build the ideal wardrobe for your lifestyle. *But it's more than that.* It's a collection of inspirational stories that serve as a reminder to listen to your inner voice and the whispers of the universe. It will inspire you to look at your wardrobe and your life from an entirely new perspective and, of course, a stylish new pair of lenses.

So, whether you struggle with your wardrobe or already have a passion for fashion and just enjoy some inspirational stories, *A Common Thread* is for you. And I am so glad you're here.

CHAPTER 1

Your Friends Are like Clothes in Your Closet

"Weave in faith, and God will find the thread."

—Saint Kabir

"I have a toast: here's to all the friends who make up my wardrobe."

I've been clinking my martini glasses to this quote for decades only to find that, twenty-five years later, this would be the catalyst for my quest in finding life's purpose and for writing this book. Why, I've wondered, have I remembered *this* adage along with so many other seemingly inconsequential, unrelated occurrences, lodged deep in my memory, since I was a child? It all felt like I was looking at an intricate clothing pattern, knowing I had all the makings of a garment but couldn't see the finished product, the proverbial runway gown. I began to pray and meditate on this thought. The more still I became, the more I was flooded with memories that were uniquely tied together by one common thread: *clothing*. I began to dive deeper into the significance of these memories and how these connections have been uniquely woven throughout my life. It soon became undeniable that each thread has had a profound impact, playing a role in the larger tapestry of my life and the lives of others.

I couldn't stop pondering on why I was recalling certain previous experiences and events; what was I supposed to do with them? Once the floodgates were opened, there was nothing I could do to stop the flow, and the stronger my desire became to unearth the significance of it all. As I began figuratively sketching and sewing each of these stories together into one, it became crystal clear: clothes have always protected, taught, and inspired me. Through the wardrobe wisdom I have accrued, which has bubbled up inside me, waiting to be put on paper, I have taken a leap of faith to share this with you and, through that process, heal.

Anaïs Nin once said, "And the day came when the risk to remain tight in a bud was more painful than the risk it took to blossom." I feel that I truly understand the meaning of this now. So, cheers to Anaïs, but more importantly, cheers to the first person who inspired me: *my dad*. My father and I didn't really have much in common except that we loved each other deeply. He grew up in a very religious home, the son of a respected and powerful chief Orthodox rabbi who came from generations of rabbis before him—ten, to be exact. His father was a prominent figure in the Orthodox community and, in 1935, started the first Hebrew parochial day school in Los Angeles, California. The Breed Street Shul (temple) was the religious and cultural pillar of the Jewish community in Boyle Heights and was nicknamed "The Queen of the Shuls."

While I didn't know my grandfather and have no memories of him (he passed away when I was three), the true "Queen of the Shul" was my Bubbie (grandmother), the *rebbetzin*. The rebbetzin is the wife of a rabbi and the female religious teacher. She was indeed one of my biggest mentors and played a huge role in my life. Although I was raised as a conservative Jew, I certainly understood the way of the Orthodox life because I spent a good majority of my childhood with my Bubbie. I couldn't wait for Fridays when we would drive to Boyle Heights where I would spend the weekend and prepare for the Sabbath with her. Being the rebbetzin of the shul was a huge undertaking, and there was a lot of preparation that went into each and every weekend. We had a routine, and for a young child without a connection to her biological mother or parental guidance (more on this later), this was extremely grounding and necessary for me.

My Bubbie's home always smelled of a mixture of Jewish foods, garlic, and old dusty books. Her home was a two-story early 1900s Craftsman–style house with a closed-eave overhang and a wide front porch, on which I would spend hours playing alone. As warm and inviting as the house was, it also had an eerie and mysterious feel; there were rooms I was actually afraid to go into.

I once heard a story that before there was a nearby *chevra kadisha* (a place where the bodies of deceased Jews are prepared for burial and where the *shomer*, or guardian, recites psalms), one of the rooms in my Bubbie's home had been used for this purpose. I'm not sure if it's a true story, but the hairs on the back of my neck would stand up every time I walked by that room.

Other parts of her home were just as haunting. She had a dark, scary basement where she stored her Passover dishes. I refused to go down there with her to retrieve them because I was convinced there were dead bodies buried underneath. With all of its hidden compartments and doors, it was the perfect house for playing hide-and-seek. That is, until it took too long to be found, and I began hearing strange noises, would become terrified, and run to my Bubbie for safety. The doors would groan at the hinge, and the floorboards creaked throughout. At the entrance of the home, there was a library that my grandfather used as his office, in which hundreds of old books from as early as the mid-1700s lined the bookshelves, supplying that "old book" smell I mentioned earlier. My *zayde* (grandfather) and Bubbie slept in two separate beds, which was common in those days. When I visited for the weekend, she would give me her bed to sleep in, because I swore I could feel his presence when I slept in his bed.

But, even with all this, I still felt safer in her home than in my own.

When I arrived at my Bubbie's on Friday mornings, she was usually in the kitchen cleaning chicken parts for her signature matzah ball soup and grinding fish by hand for her homemade gefilte fish. The comforting aroma of sweet noodle kugel and kasha varnishkes wafted throughout the kitchen. But the minute I arrived, and regardless of how much work needed to be done, my Bubbie would stop everything and whip up a few latkes for me. She used to ask me if the "maid" (my father's mistress) fed me because she thought I was too skinny and that I was being neglected. I think it was her mission to fatten me up each weekend. She would sit with me at every meal and spoon-feed me, as if I were an infant, while singing and telling me stories until every last bite was gone. She also had an avocado tree in her backyard and would feed me two or three avocados a day as a snack.

Once I was fed, she would drape a small apron on me and we would cook together in her kosher kitchen. Kosher dietary laws forbid the mixture of milk and meat products because using the milk of an animal to cook its offspring is considered inhumane. Because *milchig* and *fleishig* (milk and meat) aren't consumed together, a kosher kitchen must have two separate sets of pots, pans, plates, and silverware: one for meat and one for dairy.

I knew my way around Bubbie's kitchen, and she trusted me to set the *shabbat* table with the appropriate dishes and silverware. Her table was always full for Friday night Sabbath and Saturday *kiddush* lunch, which was served immediately after services. Every weekend, she would graciously and dutifully open her home to the mostly widowed congregants who would show up for a traditional home-cooked meal.

After we finished preparing for the Sabbath, we would walk to the kosher market to pick up some last-minute odds and ends, plus a few of my favorite treats. On the way, we would visit several homes of the temple members that could no longer attend services and drop off food or just visit to wish them a "good shabbas." She was the most highly respected member of the Jewish community but was also highly revered by her non-Jewish friends. Everyone in her community knew her and loved her. Even her non-Jewish neighbors would say "Good shabbas, rebbetzin" when we walked by. Being with her was like being with a celebrity.

Once we were showered and dressed for the Sabbath, I would stop in all the bathrooms of the home and make sure the toilet paper was torn into usable pieces (because tearing during the Sabbath is considered a forbidden category of work) and turn on the lights that would remain on over the next twenty-four hours because turning on an incandescent light violates the biblical prohibition of "igniting" a fire. All these things were done before sundown and before our guests arrived. One by one, men with *shtreimel* (black fur hats) and *tallit* (prayer shawls) would come into our home. The table would be filled with familiar old faces who were thankful to have a place to be on the Sabbath. The evening was long, and there would be singing, chanting, praying, and studying. I would rarely make it until the end, usually falling asleep on my dad's lap and waking up the next morning to the sound of crows perched outside atop telephone poles by my Bubbie's bedroom.

On Saturday morning, I could hear her in the kitchen preparing for the *kiddush* lunch, which was served, again, in her home after the Saturday morning service. The table was clean from the night before, and my Bubbie would be dressed in her best, waiting to feed me breakfast. I would, once again, begin the ritual of setting the Sabbath table for those in need. Hand in hand, we walked to shul and took our rightful seats, in the front of the women's section on the balcony of the two-story synagogue (men and women are forbidden to sit together). I sat, chanting ancient melodic prayers for three hours, most of which I didn't understand but somehow elicited a warmth and connection inside of me, nonetheless. Prayer had become a part of me, and out of all the things that my Bubbie taught me, it's been prayer and being of service that have served me the most in my life.

Although deceased, my zayde was mentioned at almost every service, and Torah study was frequently learned in his honor. After services, we walked back to Bubbie's, where another Sabbath meal was served, complete with black hats and familiar faces, followed by some cleanup, shabbat rest, and a *Havdalah* service (a ceremony that marks the end of the Sabbath).

On Sundays, we would take the bus to Fairfax, where Bubbie would buy some new shoes or clothes, which was my favorite part of the weekend. Afterward, we spent the rest of the afternoon at the Jewish Federation thrift store, where she would volunteer her time. Perhaps that is where I fell in love with heirlooms and all things vintage. I would sift through piles of old clothes, often wondering about the person who once donned these treasures, imagining who they were and what their lives were like. Sometimes, I could swear I could feel an energy to them, like a spirit that lived within. I would rummage through heaps of clothes in search of hidden treasures, like a beautiful brooch or a beaded purse. I would play dress-up for hours, creating different themed characters and curating looks. I was lost in play, and time went by so fast. I was always disappointed when it was time to leave.

This is what a typical weekend looked like at my Bubbie's, and a snapshot of how my father grew up with two of the most prominent pillars in the Orthodox community in a very religious, respected, structured, and extremely community-oriented home.

Ironically, this couldn't be further from how he raised me.

My father, instead, divorced my mother, had an affair with our young housekeeper, and raised her son. By doing so, he had disgraced his entire family, as I'm fairly certain that wasn't what they wanted for him—or even what he had intended or planned for himself.

My zayde had four children with his first wife: three daughters and a son. My Bubbie, his second wife, was only four years older than his eldest child when they wed. Their marriage allowed my Bubbie to leave Poland and escape the Holocaust, but many of her siblings and family would not be as lucky as she was. Once married, they had two children of their own, including my father and my aunt. Both my father and his stepbrother attended the Yeshiva, an Orthodox Jewish seminary, to study and become the eleventh- and twelfth-generation rabbis. While his brother did become the eleventh rabbi, my father remained uninterested in joining the clergy and would eventually break away from the Orthodox community. He was a religious man at heart, but he was torn between pleasing his family and living according to Orthodox law and maintaining a more secular lifestyle. He wrestled with his own truth, one that embraced both traditionalism and secularism, which would always be at odds with each other. My father would choose the latter, setting off a chain of events that would render my entire childhood a web of lies that we worked actively to hide from my Orthodox family and religious community.

My parents were married for eleven years, but my father's infidelity made it impossible for my mother to stay in the marriage. She decided to leave not only my father, but her three children as well. As the youngest, I was only six months old when she left, leaving my father as the sole caretaker—an overwhelming responsibility for him. My father worked long hours as a general contractor, leaving the home before 6:00 A.M. and returning late in the evenings. To help with the task of raising a family as a single parent, my father hired a beautiful and then-pregnant eighteen-year-old named Flora to live with us and help raise me and my brothers while my dad went to work to support us and make a decent living. My biological mother would later tell me that this arrangement was supposed to be temporary and that her intentions were to get "healthy" and return as a parent who could have custody of us 50 percent of the time. Neither of those things happened, and what was supposed to be a temporary job arrangement for Flora, until she gave birth to her son and we found a replacement nanny, became a more permanent nightmare that would last nineteen years. Her child, whom I consider a brother, is what I would call the only *blessing* that came out of that relationship.

It wasn't always this way, though. Flora and I were very bonded for the first eight years of my life, and I will forever hold gratitude in my heart for her nurturing me as an infant, regardless of how things ended for us. I was very attached to her, and she to me, at least during the early portion of my life. In fact, I was so attached to her that when my own mother did come to visit with me, which was very infrequent, I refused to go to her. When I wasn't with my Bubbie or aunt, I spent all my time with Flora, and there were times when I didn't even want to go to my Bubbie's because I just wanted to be with Flora.

In the beginning, Flora was protective, nurturing, and loving toward me— I even called her Mama, as she raised me from infancy. She was also very beautiful. I idolized her. Secretly, I wanted my father to fall in love and marry her so that I could officially claim her as my mother. But I knew this could never happen since his family would disown him.

To me, Flora was my surrogate mother. But to my Orthodox family, she was the maid—and that's all she ever would be. When I was with my Orthodox family and members of my religious community, I was not allowed to refer to her as "Mama" and was instructed by my father that I could only refer to her as Tia, which also means "aunt" in Spanish. The message was clear to me: I had to hide and downplay our relationship because my family would not approve. This was an emotional task that would prove difficult for both Tia and myself. I wrestled with the guilt over calling her an aunt when, in fact, she was filling the role of my mother. Even more heart-wrenching were those sporadic, unpredictable moments when my biological mom would decide to reappear, popping back into my life, and I would have to call *her* "Mom."

I don't know when my father started sleeping with Tia. I suspect a few years after she was introduced into our home, since there would be multiple housekeepers throughout my upbringing who made their way into his bed shortly after they were hired. But Tia was more than just a housekeeper; she was his mistress, the surrogate mother to his three children, and the woman of the house. Every several months, when our family would come to visit, she would move out of the master bedroom and into the maid's room in the back of the house, disappearing until they left and only appearing if she was needed to cook or clean. This must have been so degrading for her.

This would go on for years, and when she finally realized that my father's fear of losing his family was greater than his commitment to their relationship, she found a solution: alcohol and pills. My life from age eight on would never be the same. My Bubbie hated Tia and referred to her as "that woman" or "the maid" and suspected that my father might be having a relationship with her. When I went to visit her, she would ask me questions about their sleeping arrangements. To which, I was instructed to lie, but my Bubbie knew. She also suspected that Tia was hitting me because she started noticing scratches and bruises on my body. I lied about that too. The abuse from Tia was classic textbook: physical outbursts followed by an outpouring of affection. I didn't want to lose Tia's love and was afraid she would be forced to leave if I told anyone, especially my Bubbie. So, I kept the beatings secret. Bubbie despised Tia and would tell me that she was dirty and evil and corrupting my father. Tia felt equal animosity toward her and would call my Bubbie "a witch," claiming she was cruel and horrible. I often felt torn between the two of them.

Things became even more complicated because my father was raising Jacob, Tia's son (my brother), and treated him as such; that is, unless we were with my Orthodox family. This caused a lot of tension between Tia and my father, especially the longer they were together. Tia started putting pressure on my father to include her son when we went to his mother's house for the Jewish holidays. And one year, he did just that. For as generous as my Bubbie could be, she made it very clear that he was not welcome. I could hear her yelling at my father in the kitchen. All the guests could hear it too. "How dare you bring that maid's son into my home!"

It was heart-wrenching, the way he was ostracized. I loved him like a brother and wanted to protect him but didn't know how. Tia must have found out about my Bubbie's outburst and was very protective over her son. From then on, she started favoring her son and punished me each and every time I went to Bubbie's. She did this by withdrawing her love. Or, worse, by hitting me. She even took down all the pictures of me in her back bedroom, the room she never slept in, and the walls were covered with photographs of just her son. When I asked her why she didn't have any pictures of me in her room, she said, "I don't know what you're talking about." When I pressed the issue, I ended up with a bloody lip.

I stopped spending as much time on the weekend visiting with my Bubbie, as I was becoming a teenager and wanted to be with my friends. But it was mostly because every time I spent the weekend with her, I got drilled with questions about my father, and then punished by Tia when I got back.

Tia, my "mom," grew violent and angry, becoming increasingly physically, verbally, and mentally abusive toward me the older I got. My family environment became violent and combative, and the physical assaults would correlate with her frequent drinking; the more she drank, the more beatings and bruises I received. It worked in tandem. As a result of my need for attention, I began stealing, fistfighting, smoking, and skipping school. I started drinking and using drugs to cope with my emotions. She kept me in a vicious cycle of love and hate, that is, until I hit her back for the first time when I was fifteen years old. This was a turning point in our relationship. I have always said that my mother leaving me wasn't the worst thing that happened to me; it was her replacement.

The trauma I endured during my childhood made it nearly impossible for me to have healthy relationships. Lack of trust and fear ruled my teenage years, and a good part of my adulthood. I would cling to a best friend, become very codependent and possessive, and then would look for a reason to abandon the friendship before the friend could abandon me. This fear was at the core of all my feelings. What would be considered normal adolescent behavior, like the breaking up of friendships, being left out, or having to share friends, was not something I was capable of doing or coping with. I lacked the tools to navigate even these very simple growing pains. I began to detach and found myself retreating into depression, stealing, and getting into trouble with the law.

The tools I did have, though, included my creativity, my wardrobe, and my imagination. I found comfort in creating different looks within my own closet and those of my family members. I would grab my dad's jackets, my brothers' sweatshirts, hats, and gloves and would spend hours in my room just playing with my wardrobe. I should apologize (again) for cutting the necks off my brother's favorite Ton Sur Ton sweatshirts into the off-the-shoulder Madonna trend. Clothes became my escape and haven as I stumbled around, trying to navigate my own darkness. I was fascinated with dress-up and wardrobe because I could change the way I felt simply by putting on different clothes. I could be *anyone* or anything! I could transform and pretend.

My clothes became a part of my world and, in a way, protected me from the harshness and chaos within my home. This was the beginning of my fashion journey, and the path that ultimately led me here. It took thirty-five years for me to see the common thread of what God was trying to show me.

The one thing my father understood about me was this unbridled love of fashion. My father and I didn't have much in common, and I don't think he—a formerly religious man whose wife left him and who was having a decades-long affair with his housekeeper—knew the first thing about raising a daughter. But he knew how fashion made me feel and did his best to connect the dots between us through clothes. It wasn't unusual to come home and find a shirt or an outfit that he picked up in downtown LA's garment district, lying across my bed, and next to it, on my nightstand, fresh gardenias floating in a bowl of water.

One evening, when I was thirteen and in a particularly low place in my life, I retreated to my room to cry. I was struggling with my different friendships, analyzing which ones did and didn't work, whom I was going to cut out, and whom I naively felt was betraying me. In the middle of my self-pity party, I heard a knock at my door. My father came in, sat down next to me, and asked what was wrong. I explained to him my teenage girl problems as he placed his warm hand on mine and gave me my first piece of *wardrobe wisdom*, words I have never forgotten. As I matured and later expanded my love of fashion into a career as a personal stylist, I found these words even more profound.

"Jen," he said, "your friends are like clothes in your closet. You may not understand this now, but I promise you, one day you will. You will have *business clothes* that make you feel powerful and ready for success that tell the world you are serious about business. You will have *trendy clothes* that come and go with the seasons. They are new, popular, and exciting but temporary and serve a purpose. You will have *dating clothes* that can make you feel feminine and sexy. You will have *going-out clothes* that are fun and playful. You will have *classic clothes* that make up a good majority of your closet, that you might outgrow and need to update periodically. Last, you will have *comfort clothes* that you feel most comfortable in, and you can just relax and be yourself. Within those comfort clothes, you might be lucky to have found some favorite pieces that you will never get rid of because they ground you, make you feel your best when you wear them, like a favorite sweatshirt that, the longer you have it, the more comfortable it becomes."

Teary-eyed, I took in his words.

"Jennifer," he continued, "you will be lucky if you have two or even three favorite sweatshirts in your lifetime. But here's the thing. You need them all to make up your wardrobe."

He was right, and the older I got, the more profound his analogy would be, especially as I expanded my career. As a personal stylist, I have seen firsthand the power of clothing and how clothes can transform our experiences, evoking different emotions and parts of ourselves. So, too, can friends. I have friends who serve different purposes in my life and bring out the different parts of myself. I have friends who are deep and spiritual, and others who are simple and fun. Friends who are wild, and others who are conservative. I have friends who are serious, and others I can just belly-laugh with. I have friends who inspire me, and others who challenge me. Like clothes, we all have "classic" friends who have lasted decades, or "trendy" friends who come and go. And just like with clothes, I've learned what friends "look good" on me. Who brings out the best in me and which ones just don't work for my body type, *metaphorically speaking*. But I need them all to make up my personal wardrobe.

I have been blessed with several lifelong friendships that have endured the test of time and that have been through it all with me. I have seen the inextricable connections between these relationships and my own personal growth. I have had some that have challenged me beyond belief and have been my mirror, and others that have just been my rocks and lightened my heavy heart as I wrestled with my past and my own demons. These are the *favorite sweatshirts* in my wardrobe, the ones my father spoke about, and the ones I will never get rid of. I'm thankful for those—and you know who you are. Some people have music, writing, poetry; my outlet has been clothing and fashion, coupled with a lot of therapy. Without faith and fashion, I believe I would have gone down a completely different path and continued to stumble around in the dark.

Sadly, my father died of a heart attack at the age of fifty-three. If I close my eyes, I can picture him wearing his favorite comfortable, soft, blue EZ Wear cotton sweatshirt, sitting in the reclining chair that overlooked the driveway as he waited for me in the late hours of the night to come home. He wasn't perfect; nobody is. He did his best. And there is a part of me that doesn't believe he died of a heart attack. I believe he died from a broken heart from all the shame and guilt he had to live with.

When my brothers and I packed up his belongings, I found that same blue sweatshirt. I remember picking it up and smelling it, the scent of his favorite Aramis spice cologne emanating. I held it and started sobbing. I packed up all his clothes to give away to Goodwill. It was so hard to do this. Clothes can shape parts of our identity. My father cared about his appearance, and he dressed smart. I never saw him wear a sports coat without a pocket square.

As I boxed away his belongings, readying them for donation and to find new homes at the thrift store, I had a flashback of myself as a child rummaging through the thrift store with my Bubbie. I remember thinking how bizarre it was that strangers would be walking around this earth, wearing garments that were once a part of his own life experience and manifestations of his personal self-expression. I wasn't ready to let that blue sweatshirt go.

So, instead of donating it, I took that sweatshirt and gave it to my seamstress, who made pillows for my three brothers and me. As destiny would have it, today I use mine as a pincushion for my business, and although he never got a chance to see me become a successful stylist doing exactly what I have always been passionate about, I'm certain he wouldn't be one bit surprised. In fact, I think he would be proud. So, cheers, Dad—you were right. Your friends are like clothes in your closet.

What are the basics in your closet? I like to define the basics as a "time capsule" wardrobe, similar to the "best friends" category that will withstand the test of time. Those are the things you could have worn ten years ago or could wear ten years in the future, and you will still look stylish. You may have to update them periodically, but they will most likely serve you for decades. They are the foundation on which to build upon and remain perpetually chic. Of course, with anything in life, having a strong foundation is key. The trick is to keep it simple and stick to classic cuts and shapes.

The color palette for the time capsule is neutral tones: black, cream, gray, camel, navy, tan, chocolate, and white. Adding a few rich accent colors—jewel tones, such as wine, emerald green, and rust—is a great way to add a bit of color but still remain timeless. Investing in these items is where you'll get the biggest bang for your buck, but you don't have to plunk down major cash.

Pay attention to the shapes and the silhouettes rather than the labels. There are plenty of designers to choose from, at all different price points. For example, to emulate the iconic look of the Panthére Cartier watch, try Peugeot, Citizens, or Seiko. I personally don't have real diamond stud earrings because my cubic zirconia ones do the trick for me. Also, when it comes to heel height or skirt length, refer to the section on body types in Chapter 9. Wear what feels comfortable for you, while keeping the styles similar to the time capsule pictures.

I have broken down the time capsule wardrobe into sections, allocating for a maximum of ten items in each category. Scan the QR code now to watch the free live tutorial on the *essential items* needed to begin building your timeless and functional wardrobe. As we move further along the chapters, I will be referring to the time capsule and expanding on the looks. Once you have your basics, the outfit possibilities are endless!

CHAPTER 2

You Only Lose
What You Cling To

"Nothing real can be threatened. Nothing unreal exists.
Herein lies the peace of God."

—A COURSE IN MIRACLES

Clothes can transform our lives from the outside in. They can help us gain confidence, uplift our mood, enhance our experiences, evoke emotions, improve our chances for success, and even connect us to past memories with our loved ones.

However, true transformation can't happen simply by changing your outfit alone—that requires deep inner work. Clothes and fashion are just tools to help you improve your state of mind. But there's a fine line between allowing clothes to work with and for us and allowing clothes to *define* us.

It's imperative to our overall well-being that we don't hide behind our clothes or use labels to make us feel superior, forming strong attachments to our material things. As fun as it can be to wear something new and don the latest fashion trends, there is always more to buy; trust me, it's never-ending. I have shopped in the world's most luxurious stores, surrounded by the most coveted clothes, shoes, bags, jewelry, accessories, art, and cars. It's easy to get sucked in and, I must admit, I have. Balancing my inner world and my outer world requires both awareness and attention.

In the past, I have used purchasing clothes to fill a void and, let me assure you, that euphoric feeling is temporary at best, creating a false sense of identity. I had formed strong attachments to my material things, only to find them repeatedly stripped away throughout my life. This led me to distrust almost everyone, covet more, and further attach myself to my material things, only to find them stolen once again. I couldn't understand why this kept happening to me.

What I couldn't see then was that the universe was once again weaving another thread into the fabric of my unique life's purpose. In retrospect, these were lessons I needed to learn in order to be on this career path and find a balance between the material world and my inner world. Over time, having my valuables repeatedly stolen eventually forced me to stop attaching my material things to my self-worth and to stop taking my outer world so seriously. I started developing a healthier relationship with my material possessions, but as my career flourished, I soon found myself putting too much value once again on my "things." I was gently reminded by a serendipitous encounter with a monk, who helped me fully understand how to consciously let go of attachments and grasp this ancient Zen Buddhist philosophy: "You only lose what you cling to."

As a teenager, I placed a lot of value on material things. Like most teenagers, I coveted the latest trends and wanted to fit in and be popular. I had an innate sense of style, but my family couldn't afford designer clothes. Even though I could curate some great looks on a budget, I desperately wanted designer trends and labels to feel like I fit in with the popular crowd at school. So, when I was twelve, I started working at the swap meet to be able to afford a few of the trendiest pieces. I worked every weekend and saved up my money to buy the most coveted designer items, like a Ton Sur Ton sweatshirt or a pair of Marciano Guess jeans.

I was a smart shopper, and when a style reemerged (because they always do), I could find a similar style at a vintage store and mix them in with my new trendy labels. One of my favorite pieces was a white leather fringe jacket that I purchased from a secondhand store on Melrose Avenue, right after I saw the lead actress wearing it in *Ferris Bueller's Day Off.* I loved pairing this jacket with my Guess jeans and white ankle booties.

Another favorite of mine was a buttery, leather, studded, cropped moto jacket I found in London when I was eighteen years old, which drew attention every time I wore it. My confidence would soar from the positive attention, so much so that my identity was almost exclusively built around the external and material things I had. But because of this, I failed to enhance my *inner* self. I didn't believe I had any other redeeming qualities and felt that I could hide my insecurities behind my clothes. Those insecurities, coupled with the need for attention I was desperately seeking from my father, ignited the perfect storm.

Eventually, the money I made from the swap meet wasn't enough to feed my new clothing addiction, so I began to steal in order to have the latest trends. I had been arrested several times for shoplifting and, let me advise you, it is *not* a good idea to try to outrun a police officer. I was tackled to the ground, handcuffed, and taken to Juvenile Hall. Hence, my earning the title *juvenile delinquent*. I would steal from my siblings, my father, Tia, my friends, my friends' parents, department stores—pretty much anyone and everyone except for my Bubbie and my aunt, who had always protected me. Each time I stole, a part of myself became further emotionally detached, until I felt completely numb. I was becoming spiritually bankrupt. What I didn't know then was the karmic cycle I had started and how another thread was being sewn into the story of my life.

When I was thirteen years old, my father asked me to come into his room and sit down on the edge of his bed. It was the morning of my bat mitzvah, and he handed me a box wrapped with pink ballerina paper topped with a glittery gold bow. I could tell by his facial expression and the gentle tone in his voice that whatever he was about to give me was important to him. He placed his warm hand in mine and said he was proud of me and that he blamed himself for my recent troubles. He told me how much he loved and adored me and that he wanted to be the first man to give me jewelry. I could see his eyes well up as he carefully chose his words. I opened the box, and inside was a delicate, dainty ring with my Hebrew initials etched in cursive with a small diamond in the center. Next to the ring was a gold heart-shaped locket with two intertwined hearts and, inside, a picture of the two of us.

I started to cry because of its sentiment. I felt seen and loved by my father, and out of all the things I owned, these two pieces became my most

valued possessions. Six months later, they would both disappear. I was devastated and had looked everywhere, but to no avail. I knew that I wouldn't
have lost them and was completely flabbergasted. I asked Tia and the new
housekeeper and everyone I knew if they had seen them. I searched everywhere I could think of, retraced every step, but they were nowhere to be
found. They just simply disappeared.

About a year later, my first boyfriend gave me an emerald gold ring;
shortly after he gave it to me, it, too, suddenly vanished. Then my clothes
started to disappear. That favorite Ton Sur Ton sweatshirt and my Guess
jeans that I had worked all summer at the swap meet to buy? Gone! The
repeated disappearing of my valuables felt violating, but more than that,
I felt like pieces of my identity were being stripped from me. I would lose my
confidence, and I would have to start all over again to rebuild my self-esteem
and my wardrobe, which were so strongly intertwined. I started wondering if
it was karma and decided I would never steal again.

But things continued to vanish for years. In my own blind frustration
and attachment to materialism, I started looking for other culprits, starting
with our new nineteen-year-old housekeeper, Elisa. But she kept a deadbolt
on her bedroom door, and I couldn't search her room. When inquiring why
she kept her door locked, she told me it was because she was petrified of
Tia (the woman who raised me; also, my father's mistress of nineteen years).
Tia despised Elisa and was extremely cruel to her. Unbeknownst to me, the
reason for this was because Elisa and my father were having an affair, and
Tia knew it. Could you imagine living in the same house with your lover,
knowing that he's having an affair with the housekeeper? This drove Tia to
drink even more. I once came home to find her inebriated and passed out on
the couch in the living room.

With Tia temporarily incapacitated, I suddenly got the idea to search
the master bedroom for my missing things. As I was looking through the
drawers, I found the combination to a safe and immediately got a pit in
my stomach. It's as if I already knew. I quickly found the safe in the closet
and dialed the combination. My hands were trembling as I turned the dial
back and forth, fearful that she would wake up at any minute. I could feel

my heart pounding out of my chest. It took me several tries to open it, but I finally heard the safe click open. I pulled on the handle and began looking through the jewelry boxes and—*lo and behold!*—there they were. Tia had, indeed, stolen my jewelry.

I was in complete shock and disbelief. Scrambling for coherency, I stood frozen in the dimly lit closet for what seemed like an eternity. I could not comprehend why the woman who raised me, the woman I considered my mother, would steal from me. Suddenly I was jolted into reality when I heard the front door slam. I quickly put everything back, except for my jewelry (which I reclaimed), and I closed the safe. I didn't have time to search for my clothes, but now I knew that I wasn't crazy. I also knew that I could never trust anyone ever again. I eventually told my father about my jewelry, but he didn't believe me. Tia denied it and said that I was the thief in the house. Of course, with my past record, my father believed Tia. She loved to remind him that I was a juvenile delinquent and a liar. We didn't speak much after that, although we continued living in the same house, in parallel worlds.

A few days later, I tried to snoop in Tia's room again to reclaim more of my belongings, but she must have figured out that I had found my jewelry and put a deadbolt over her closet doors. I eventually put a deadbolt on my door too, but over the years, things somehow continued to vanish from my room. My white fringe jacket and the buttery leather London moto were nowhere to be found. I had to constantly remember to lock my door, even if I was leaving my room to spend time in other parts of my own home. And it wasn't just my clothes that were stolen—after a sleepover, my friends' clothes would suddenly disappear too.

It seemed like a never-ending cycle. It was so frustrating and embarrassing that some of my friends stopped wanting to spend the night. Every time I saved up my money and bought myself something that I loved and became attached to it, it would eventually disappear. Once again, I felt like pieces of my identity were being stripped from me.

The closer I was to graduating high school, the more I wanted out. Tia's drinking also escalated to a new level, and I would periodically come home from school to find random men in my home drinking with her. They would peer at me like a piece of meat, such that I never felt protected and safe in the confines of my own home, even with a deadbolt over my door. Fear plagued me like an invisible intruder. I needed to escape this nightmare, and when one of my childhood best friends Jenny Stein called and told me she was moving to San Diego to attend junior college, I packed my bags and left a few weeks later. I told my father I would return when Tia was gone.

Several months later, I got a phone call from my father. Tia had left him for good. Incidentally, she met a neighbor and ran off to marry him. My roommate and I decided to come home for a surprise visit. Since I had left for college, my father had suffered a heart attack and needed to reduce his stress. To help generate some income, he rented out all the bedrooms in our home except for the maid's room and the master bedroom.

When we arrived that night, I had forgotten that my room was being occupied by one of the renters. Elisa graciously offered her room to us and said she would sleep on the couch downstairs. The next morning, I woke up at the crack of dawn in Elisa's bed, disoriented. It took me a few minutes to remember where I was. I lay there staring straight ahead at the two mirrored closets facing me. The sunrise cast a warm glow in the room and shone a ray of light into the opening of one of the sliding closet doors. It took me a minute for my eyes to adjust and for my mind to register what appeared in front of me. I sat up in the bed and leaned forward to get a better view of what I had been staring at. Hanging in the closet was my *favorite* white fringe jacket I had been missing for years and, next to it, the buttery leather one I had purchased in Europe—both of which had mysteriously vanished.

I quickly got out of bed and opened the closet doors. I couldn't believe my eyes. Dozens of shirts, jackets, and pants that belonged to me and my friends were nestled among her wardrobe. I looked under the bed, and *more* clothes were hidden there. I searched in and around the nightstands, and when I moved the bedside tables to look behind them, something was protruding from inside the wall. It looked like fabric was coming out of it, and it was then that I understood what Elisa had done.

She had taken an electric saw and drilled a hole into the drywall and shoved my lingerie into the hole. As I started pulling out my bras, underwear, and lace negligees, I found an envelope with a key and some photographs of her and my father together. In the photographs, Elisa was wearing *my* lingerie. I had to hold the photo closer to my face because, in the dimly lit room, she looked exactly like me. I was disgusted. Tia was right: my father *was* having an affair with her. I piled the clothes onto the foot of the bed and began crying hysterically. All this time, I thought Tia had stolen my clothes.

I stared at the pictures in utter disbelief and held the key in the palm of my hand, wondering what it was for. Then a light bulb went off in my head. I walked across the hall and quietly slid the key into the deadbolt of my bedroom door and heard it click open. I felt violated and betrayed once again, and all the old feelings rushed back. I suddenly felt all alone in the world, standing there in the hall knowing that my father would once again choose Elisa over me, just like he had chosen Tia. All the memories of my childhood came flooding back to me: the abuse I endured, the lies I grew up with, the secrets I had to keep, the drugs and alcohol—and I realized that I could never return home again. My father simply replaced Tia with Elisa, and this would never end. He would cheat on Elisa too, and she would be a woman scorned, just like Tia.

That morning was a turning point for me, one where, I think, I was forced to grow up. I vowed to myself that I'd never return home. My childhood best friend Jen sat beside me, like she always did, holding me and assuring me that I would be all right. I wanted to fall to the ground and sob like a child. I felt like I was drowning; I needed a life vest. I wanted something to fill the emptiness inside of me. I felt scared and alone. I closed my eyes as she stroked my hair, and I did the only thing I knew to do at that moment: I prayed. I prayed for the chaos to stop, for a normal life where I could feel safe and protected, and to finally find peace.

Three years later, I met Tony and my prayers were answered. Tony was the ray of light into my darkness, and I'll remember my wedding day as one of the happiest days of my life. My love for styling even has its roots in being a bride: I had dreamed about my wedding day since I was a little girl and can't count how many times I played dress-up, pretending to be a bride. I wore a tiara to my sixth-grade graduation with a white, tiered fit-and-flare dress.

My homecoming and prom dresses all looked like wedding gowns, adorned with pearl embellishments, satin trim, and tulle. If I could have worn a veil without scaring off my dates in high school, trust me, I would have. When I dreamed about my fairy-tale wedding as a young girl, I wanted to look like a princess with a tulle gown and a tiara that resembled a crown, an ice sculpture of two doves kissing, tall white floral centerpieces with enormous candelabras, a huge all-white rose floral wedding canopy with bistro lights, and, of course, my Prince Charming—all of which, I can say, did come true.

But the one thing I didn't envision was that my father would not be there to give me away, and so for the one small, poignant moment, there was an indelible moment of sadness. My father was waiting for a heart transplant and, sadly, passed away before finding a donor. Once again, something—or in this case, *someone*—so valuable was taken from me suddenly and without warning. Despite such a devastating loss, my wedding was absolutely perfect. I walked down that aisle without any reservations. I knew I was marrying my soul mate. And I would marry him all over again—in fact, *I have*. We have had several vow renewals. We were even remarried by an Elvis impersonator at the infamous Vegas Wedding Chapel on our five-year anniversary.

But it was our twenty-five-year wedding anniversary in Aspen that has been the most memorable of all my weddings. I wore a simple, elegant, sheer white Ronny Kobo dress with a diamond-encrusted vintage brooch, gifted to me by my mother-in-law, and a pair of art deco vintage chandelier earrings my husband bought me in New York.

My two sons gave me away, and each held my arm as they walked me through a path of gardenias, the flowers my father used to leave by my bedside. As the guitar player strummed to the tune of Leonard Cohen's "Hallelujah" and my sons stood by, one on each side of me, there wasn't one moment of sadness. I could feel my father's presence that day. Nestled among the majestic snow-capped mountains and next to a glistening stream, the four of us held hands as we exchanged vows and were guided through a spiritual renewal. To complete the ceremony, I had Mala necklaces made for Tony, me, and each of our boys. A Mala necklace is a string of prayer beads used in various world religions and dates back to the eighth century

BCE. Each gemstone was intentionally hand-picked to represent each of the unique roles we have played in our family and serves as a reminder of our bond and unconditional love for one another.

The boys all have lava stones to connect them, a reminder to create consciously and harmoniously and to stand together—to provide for the family and assert gentle strength and true love. All our Malas have a citrine stone that symbolically binds us. Citrine is the stone of the sun and represents radiance and power, the ability to give life and provide nourishment to all beings. A reminder to fill up with the light of the commitment to a love that stands the test of time. Tony's necklace has a tourmaline pendant to remind him of his strength and capacity to love, guide, and trust. My necklace has a silk tassel to remind me of my wisdom and grace, labradorite for protection, moonstone for balance, and a tigereye to know my strength.

Having these pieces made for us was an integral part of the renewal for me and a tangible family heirloom that can now be passed down through generations. They hold intrinsic value that connects us all to the memory of this special day and would be irreplaceable if stolen. But, of course, with such precious jewelry, I could feel old habits coming back. Thankfully, while some wounds can't be healed, they can be reduced to a manageable size. Upon getting them, I suddenly became paranoid. For the most part, I was able to manage my fears that I would, once again and without explanation, lose something important to me. But once in a while, those feelings would surface surreptitiously, like a dark cloud on a sunny day.

It had been years since I had these unsafe feelings. Because of my paranoia, I drove the boys crazy during our trip, reminding them to put the bracelets in a safe place if they took them off and to make sure that they were securely fastened. They would always respond, asking, "Who would steal these bracelets?" to which I would reply, "Anyone, given the opportunity."

These thoughts became all-consuming, and I wanted to go for a walk to clear my head. So, Tony and I headed into the small town of Aspen and stumbled upon a beautiful museum, one we were initially drawn to because of its unique modern architecture. The all-glass, four-story contemporary structure was vastly different from the surrounding buildings. We were captivated by the way it stood out among the majestic, natural surroundings of the pine trees and the snow-capped mountain peaks.

Upon entering the museum, we were greeted by its curator and handed a pamphlet with a description of the exhibits on each floor. As we entered the elevator, she said to make sure that we visit the fourth floor where the monks would be finishing up the mandala. To be honest, I didn't even know what a mandala was, but I was curious. Turns out, Buddhist monks spend their lives going from place to place, making these sacred cosmograms that originated over 2,500 years ago, called *mandalas*. They're composed of millions of pieces of vivid sand colors. The monks use metal funnels called *chak-purs* to pick up the colored grains and then tap the end of the metal tools to strategically place the sand, creating elaborate patterns on the pieces of wood.

It's quite stunning to see in person, but the most fascinating part is the amount of patience required to perform this intricate process. Depending on the size of the mandala, this meticulous process could take a few days to several weeks to complete just one. The monks bend over the piece for hours on end, dropping one grain of sand after another into intricate, ancient symbolic patterns.

I stood behind the roped-off area and watched in awe as the monks silently and harmoniously created these beautiful, complicated sand paintings with such focus and grace. I stood until I became restless and recognized the feelings of my own anxiety mixed, oddly, with a deep reverence. I thought, *How could one be so disciplined for such a long period?* Then I thought about their burgundy robes and wondered if they ever wanted to wear secular clothing and how vastly different our worlds were. I wanted to know more about them and their way of life. The monks worked for several hours at a time and then took shifts, so I waited for one of the shifts to end, and that's when I met Shenzu.

Shenzu had one of the kindest faces I had ever seen. His eyes struck me first. They were murky with age yet still held a vibrant sparkle. His pupils were pierced with wisdom, inviting and warm. His smile was simple but unforgettable, and his calm demeanor immediately put me at ease. I had this peculiar feeling that he had known me, like he knew what I was going to ask and what I needed to hear. I listened to his every word as he told me the ways of Tibetan culture. He had been a monk since he was eight years old, and in the Tibetan monastery, monks studied their entire lives, earning the equivalent of a doctoral degree.

He told me that monks are students for life and that the word for *monk* is "trapa," which means "student." A monk's life begins at 2:00 A.M. with morning prayer, after which they spend up to nine hours a day in private prayer and meditation, in addition to their studies. I learned about their *kashaya* robes and how they symbolize simplicity and detachment of materialism. The reason they shave their heads is to show humility and religious devotion. When I asked Shenzu about how he generated income, he told me that monks are reliant on the lay community to provide for them and, in return, the monasteries provide guided meditation, spiritual support, and ceremonies.

I was fascinated and listened intently to his every word. I wanted to know more about the mandala. He said that one must be educated for three years in the philosophical significance and symbolism before being allowed to make one, as the very act of creating a mandala is believed to be sacred. The four corners represent the four immeasurables in Buddhism: lovingkindness, compassion, altruistic joy, and equanimity. Throughout the sand painting, there are numerous symbols that all have specific and significant meaning. His group had been traveling for the last year, creating mandalas and had been at this museum for the last six days, working from morning until night on this particular one.

It was then that I had what I thought was a brilliant idea. Could I buy the mandala so the monks could use the money for food or future travel? When I proposed my idea, he smiled and said that I was too kind, but that the mandala can't be sold; after its completion, it had to be destroyed. *But why?* I asked. I couldn't comprehend why or *how* they could ruin something so beautiful that took endless hours to create.

He grinned in a way that a wise teacher would look at a young, innocent child, as if to say, You still have so much to learn.

"The mandala represents the human journey from ignorance to enlightenment," Shenzu explained. "It signifies the ultimate impermanence of all conditioned things. There is a beginning and an end to everything. We must let go of attachments because the root of suffering *is* attachment."

"How do I enjoy anything without being attached to it? Do I just go through life without caring about anything?" I asked, confused.

"To be detached doesn't mean being indifferent. It means deep involvement in life, but there is a lack of attachment to the outcome," he replied. "It's about finding peace through letting go."

This shot right through me. I could feel the electricity from every hair in my body stand up. Then and there, I had an epiphany: my fears were directly proportional to my attachments. I lived in fear of having things taken from me. I feared that my father, my husband, my friendships, my material things, my ideas, and my creativity would all be taken away or stolen from me—and if that happened, how would I ever recover? I was trying to *avoid* fear. But what if I lived life without the fear of the outcome? What if I just lived fully *in* the moment, without holding myself back? How much more of life could I inhale and what kinds of things could I experience? And how?

I revealed to Shenzu my fear of things being stolen from me and that I thought this was holding me back from finding my purpose. I told him I could hear the universe whispering, but I was afraid; I was afraid of sharing my ideas because I was fearful someone would take what's mine. Shenzu listened, smiled with his eyes, and said, "You only lose what you cling to."

I lay awake all night thinking about my conversation with Shenzu and how his words and voice had comforted my wounds. I thought about how all the things I had clung to were, indeed, taken from me. I thought about how nothing is permanent except for our experiences and our memories. I closed my eyes and pictured myself sitting on the edge of my father's bed and the words he said to me on my thirteenth birthday. I could feel his deep melodic voice reverberate through my soul, and I felt a calm and a peace flow through me. I may not have the locket or the gold ring, but I would always have the memory of how he made me feel that day. I thought about visiting my brother in London and the fun we had roaming the streets together where I found that buttery leather jacket. How I wouldn't trade that experience for anything and how I will always have that memory, even though that jacket is now long gone. I thought about the boys' Mala bracelets and realized that, even if they were lost or stolen, the memory of that magical day will be embedded within us forever. I thought about my father's death and how nothing had been taken away from me. He lives on within me, through my memories of him. We have no control over when or how someone dies. We only have control over how we live in the moment.

I thought about the fate of meeting Shenzu and that, despite how vastly different our worlds were, his wisdom made me into a better stylist. And while I'm certainly not ready to live like a monk and let go of my materialism, today I am even more conscientious of wasteful spending and utilizing what we already own. We don't always need to buy labels or overspend to look great or to feel confident. I try to remind myself and my clients not to allow clothes to define us or to form strong attachments to our things.

The next morning, we went back to the museum to see the closing ritual ceremony of the mandala. A small crowd gathered silently around the roped-off areas that surrounded the sacred cosmogram. The monks dressed in ceremonial fashion, which consisted of an additional piece of fabric worn across their shoulders, like harnesses, adorned with ancient symbols and intricate headdresses. Several of the monks had special musical instruments. I could see Shenzu through the crowd and hoped that he might look up to see me among the spectators. It was a silly thought because, of course, he was fully focused on the dismantling of the mandala. The service began with low rhythmic chanting, followed by a soft ringing of bells. A melodic drumroll followed, and then the piercing sound of an oboe reverberated throughout the museum.

Suddenly, and in one quick, graceful swoop, the mandala was destroyed, dissolved into piles of sand. We watched as the monks scooped up piles of formless grains into an urn. Once all the sand was gathered into the vessel, they formed a procession and headed to the Roaring Fork River to be dispersed. I watched the sand float through the air, like thousands of pieces of glitter, as they settled on the top of the turquoise-blue river and were quickly swept away by the current. It reminded me of human ashes being scattered to free the soul or spirit back to where it came from. I imagined the sand being my fear, carried away by the current, and I felt it leave my body.

There are moments that transform us from one moment to the next. This was one of those moments. I decided right then and there that I would no longer let my fear hold me back from what the universe had been whispering to me all this time. That night, *A Common Thread* was born.

CHAPTER 3

Take a Trip
Down Memory Lane

*"It is not what we see and touch or that which others do for us
which makes us happy; it is that which we think and feel and do,
first for the other fellow and then for ourselves."*

—Helen Keller

Sometimes things just simply go out of style, and it's time to let them go. But what about the notion that everything eventually comes back into style, and how do we know if it's worth hanging on to these emblematic old trends for decades? In the following chapters, we're going to begin the process of *letting go*, but before we begin weeding out what's not serving us, I have my own theory about what stands the test of time, and this chapter is about knowing what to keep and *why*. I happen to love heirlooms and vintage pieces because they have an energy of their own and often hold sentimental value. They can also offer a glimpse into someone's history or a family tradition.

I have a great eye for finding a diamond in the rough. Tucked away in a jewelry drawer or hidden in a client's closet, I will inevitably find an unworn heirloom or a vintage treasure piece. It has become one of my goals while working in a client's closet to incorporate these sentimental pieces into their updated lookbooks: a 1920s art deco earring, a Czech festoon opal necklace from the '40s, a vintage brooch, a tweed Chanel blazer, or a fur coat from Bullocks of Wilshire are just a few of the hidden treasures I've found lurking in the dusty corners of some of my clients' wardrobes.

What I love most about heirlooms or vintage pieces is the *history* behind each piece—or, sometimes, the mystery of the untold stories behind them. One day, hopefully, I'll have a granddaughter who will inherit one of my most treasured heirlooms: an original Judith Leiber oblong-shaped evening bag gifted to me by my mother-in-law for my fiftieth birthday (proudly shown in the cover photo). Judith Leiber's bags have been carried for decades by renowned women, including First Ladies, princesses, celebrities, wives of Soviet leaders, and even Queen Elizabeth II. Her whimsical bedazzled hand-bags are known for their multicolored rhinestones and for being encrusted in Swarovski crystals. They are both tactile and beautiful visual displays of art.

When I would visit my mother-in-law, I would peruse her closet and covet the eye-catching creation displayed in her étagère. I would carefully take it out of its original dust bag and box and run my fingers over its color-ful beads, admiring its beauty. She would always say, "One day, everything I have will be yours," which made me feel uncomfortable at the thought of her not being here one day but also very grateful to have something of sentimental value that I could pass down to future generations.

On *November 24*, the actual day of my fiftieth birthday, she and I had breakfast together. Afterward, she looked at me and said that she had a very hard time deciding what to buy me for my birthday because she wanted me to have something special and meaningful that I could always remember to mark the significance of this monumental birthday. She said that rather than waiting until she's no longer here on earth, she would much rather reap the joy of seeing me use something that belonged to her, that carried with it a very special place in her heart. She told me that her late husband (and the love of her life) gave it to her, and she wanted me to have it. I reached into the gift bag and carefully pulled out the box. I recognized it and began sobbing, as I knew immediately what was inside. I was flooded with over-whelming emotion: for the first time in my life, I felt like a real daughter. I opened the box and, with tears running down my face, there it was: the Judith Leiber bag, enveloped in its original cloth and packaging.

"All the original paperwork is inside, honey," she said. "I think he pur-chased it in New York on Madison Avenue."

I pulled out the original receipt and carefully unfolded it and gasped. The sales receipt read:

Name: Joseph Brown
Style# Mn31314j3 g / multi Panache bag
Date: November 24th, 1999

Unknown to both of us, he had purchased the bag on my exact birthday, twenty-one years earlier! She looked at me, my face still streaked with tears, and said that, somehow, she knew in her heart that she needed to give it to me.

Wardrobe and jewelry can remind us of our past and can also connect us to the people we once loved. Sometimes we know the stories of those who wore them, such as in the case of my birthday bag, and the significance of those treasured pieces; sometimes we don't.

I know that if I just sat in my own closet, I could take a trip down memory lane. My wardrobe is like an accumulation of memories and remnants of other people's pasts, each piece evoking an emotion. As my eyes scan my closet, I know certain pieces represent such vivid memories and hold such sentimental value that merely *looking* at them is as if I've traveled back in time.

When I wear the diamond-encrusted flower vintage brooch my grandmother gave me, it's almost as if I feel her energy surrounding me with love: I am connected to her. I still smile when I see the YAYA halter top I was wearing when my husband and I first fell in love, when we stayed up all night talking until the sun came up. How proud I feel when I peruse my dresses and see the Alexander McQueen and Pucci dresses I wore to my sons' bar mitzvahs.

Other pieces in my closet have sadder memories, like the Laura Ashley sweater tucked away in the corner that once belonged to my sister-in-law, who took her life, or the coat I wore to my father's funeral. My closet is full of clothes that make up different chapters in my life, filled with the pages and pages of memories that go with them.

At the end of my closet is a window where the natural sunlight shines through, and just outside is a beautiful old oak tree. When I can, I love to just sit on my velvet tufted ottoman and stare outside. Just below the window is a built-in dresser with some trinkets and various things I've accumulated throughout my life: a black leather-bound box with a brass duck on it that belonged to my father, inside of which contains a few of his favorite silk pocket squares. Next to that box is a mirrored tray with a few vintage perfume bottles, two Swarovski ballerina dancers given to me by each of my sons, and a music box that my father gave me when I turned thirteen years old. Next to that is a picture of my son and a Holocaust survivor, where they are both smiling. My son Drew stands next to Henry, the survivor, who has his arm proudly stretched out toward the camera, bearing the numbers B-7648, a permanent reminder of a horrific past. On Henry's right wrist, he proudly shows off his new leather bracelet, a representation of kindness and love. This bracelet represents the true spirit of giving and receiving and how one small act of kindness can truly change the trajectory of many lives.

When Drew was seventeen years old, he unexpectedly announced that he wanted to join the US Army. This news came to us as quite a shock because he had never shown any interest in being in the military before. I have so much respect for the men and women who serve our country, but this wasn't something I thought was the right choice for our son. When I asked him why he wanted to serve, he said he wanted to find meaning in his life and that he felt empty. Drew was a good student but has always been frustrated with the educational system, and his academic work felt meaningless.

He felt his friendships were lacking depth and meaning, and he had no idea what he wanted to do with his future. So, being of service to our country seemed like a logical solution to him. Now, I'm not sure this is a typical thing most kids his age struggle with, but then again, there is nothing typical about Drew. I have always felt like he is an old soul. After all, he comes from a long lineage—ten generations, actually—of Orthodox rabbis who spent their lives searching and interpreting the Bible and the meaning of life. It's literally in his genes.

We weren't sure how to answer some of the very deep questions he was asking us and would respond with answers like, "You don't need to figure it out now. You're doing great—just relax and don't stress about your future so much. Have faith in God and in yourself." As parents, this was our way of trying to assuage his youthful but valid fears.

But our advice only made him more frustrated. We tried to encourage him to find hobbies or to be of service to others, but that only made what he was feeling seem even more esoteric and isolating. We could see that he was withdrawing into his room more and spending less time with his friends. He started developing insomnia and became depressed. It was as if he were a prisoner, trapped by his own thoughts.

One evening, I went into his room before retiring for the night and sat down on his bed to talk. I talked to him about what I like to refer to as a "God shot"—when happenings appear to bear the fingerprints of the divine providence. I have had many of them throughout my life, and this is a story about one particular instance that changed the course of Drew's life. That night, I told my younger son that when I felt lost and needed direction, I would pray and then quiet my mind and listen. I would listen with my ears *and* my eyes. The answer would eventually come.

The answers often feel to me like a strong inspirational thought, a gut feeling, a creative urge, a visceral knowing, a universal force, or an inside voice that all bear the fingerprints of something much bigger than any of us. In my experience, the real key, though, is that once you receive the feeling, you must act on it. This is where most people fail to get the message. Most of us get into FEAR (false evidence appearing real) and lack the will to move forward. I told him he would know when he gets a God shot because once he acts on it, it will feel like preordained synchronicity, as if the universe is conspiring and pushing things in motion. It's like swimming downstream with the current.

You never really know what sinks in with your children. To be honest, I didn't think he really heard a word I was saying that night when I sat on his bed. I leaned over, gave him a hug and a kiss, and went to bed. Several weeks later, on a Friday morning, Drew came into my room before leaving for school and said, "Mom, look what I found."

He stretched out his arm and on his wrist was a leather bracelet that he purchased in Jerusalem when he was thirteen years old. He wore this bracelet religiously for several years but had misplaced it. Etched into the leather was a Hebrew inscription of the Shema Y'srael, the prayer that serves as the centerpiece of the morning and evening prayer service. It translates to: "Hear, O Israel: the Lord is our God, the Lord is one." Drew was thrilled he had found it again. So, with his bracelet back on his wrist, he headed off to school unaware that there would be a Holocaust survivor speaking at the monthly school assembly that day.

Henry told his personal and very tragic story of his survival of the Holocaust during World War II, where 6 million Jews were massacred. His family was taken abruptly from Germany when he was just thirteen and put into a ghetto with his mother and father. When they were transported to the first concentration camp, his father was forced to work long, arduous hours with minimal food. Within a short time, he died of starvation, in Henry's arms no less.

When Henry was fifteen, he and his mother were transported to Auschwitz, the most notorious concentration camp and known for inhumanely exterminating their prisoners via gas chambers. Upon their arrival, Henry was separated from his mother; sadly, it would be the last time he would ever see her.

Henry told his heart-rending and tragic story of survival that day in an auditorium filled with high school students. Drew said you could hear a pin drop. After the assembly, Henry said that he would remain in the auditorium during lunch if anyone wanted to ask him any further questions. Drew, who was touched and intrigued by his story, stayed in the auditorium to hear more. He listened as students asked him various questions like, "Were you afraid?" and "How long did you go without food?"

And then there was one question that would change the trajectory of both Henry's and Drew's lives.

"Have you ever been to Israel?" asked one student.

"Unfortunately, that is my one regret," Henry replied, sadly.

"Why don't you go now?" the student pressed.

"Well, I'm eighty-nine years old, and it's just a little too late for that now," he said.

At that moment, Drew looked down at his bracelet and the gut feeling came in—an inspiration to do something, a knowing. Drew hesitated for a moment as he wondered if the other students would judge him and think he was being weird. But upon remembering our conversation, he listened to his inner voice and took a leap of faith. He walked up to Henry, took off his bracelet, stretched out his hand, and said, "I got this when I was in Jerusalem, the holiest city in Israel. I would like you to have it. If you're not going to go to Israel, then this is a way to have a piece of Israel with you."

Henry was very taken aback at this gesture and apprehensive at first. It was clear that he felt uncomfortable accepting a gift from a teenager he didn't know, but to whom he had revealed a deeply personal tragedy, nonetheless. He said he never had anyone offer him something like this. Drew could tell Henry was trying not to get emotional.

"Oh, no, I can't accept this," said Henry.

"I really want you to have it. It would mean a lot to me," Drew replied.

Reluctantly, Henry accepted the bracelet. The school bell rang, and Drew headed off to his next class. He called me after school and told me what he had done, and I remember my eyes filling up with tears. I was so proud of his generous and kind heart.

Later that week, Henry contacted the school asking if he could have Drew's phone number because he wanted to get in touch with him to thank him once again for the bracelet. Several days later, Henry called and asked Drew to join him for lunch. Henry was very touched by Drew's gesture; he wanted Drew to know that he has spoken to hundreds of schools for over twenty years and had never had anyone touch his heart the way that Drew did. Over a lunch meeting, it became clear that the two shared a unique soul connection; it would be the beginning of a special friendship.

One afternoon, Drew came home and said that Henry wanted to meet me and asked me if I wanted to join them for lunch. I was thrilled to meet Henry, and that following week the three of us met at Henry's favorite restaurant, King's Fish House. Upon meeting Henry, I was surprised at who I saw: a tall and robust gentleman, eighty-nine years young, with the vigor, energy, and mental astuteness of someone much younger.

We started lunch with the ordinary exchange of banter, but as our meal progressed, Henry began opening up more about his past. Drew and I became very intrigued with parts of his story that we weren't initially aware of. First, we found out that Henry was a German Jew and that his father tried desperately, on numerous occasions, to give him a bar mitzvah in the ghetto when they were taken from their home. A bar mitzvah is a Jewish tradition that marks the passage from boyhood to manhood when a boy reaches the age of thirteen. Sadly, Henry's father wasn't able to give him this treasured rite of passage before he died; Henry never had one.

We also learned that Henry lost all his family members in the Holocaust, but that he still had one living relative whom he had never met who lived in Israel. And, on a strange note, we found out that Yad Vashem, the most prominent Holocaust remembrance museum in Israel, had erroneously indicated that Henry had perished in the Holocaust.

And finally, we learned that the chief Orthodox rabbi of Israel, Rabbi Israel Meir Lau, was one of the fifteen boys who was liberated with Henry when he was just eight years old; they had not seen or spoken to each other since. We were dumbfounded upon learning all these things about Henry's story, which started to feel like an unfinished poem, the missing verses of which could be found in the Holy Land. As Henry shared these things with us, I could see the wheels spinning in Drew's head as he was getting another God shot. The minute we got into the car, he looked over at me and said enthusiastically, "Mom, I have to do something. I have to get Henry to Israel. He needs to meet his cousin and have a bar mitzvah." He added, "Maybe we could even get in touch with the museum and tell them that Henry is alive, and have his records changed."

"Okay, so what do you want to do, Drew?" I asked him, beaming with pride at his revelation.

"I don't know. What can we do?" he asked back.

"Why don't we do a fundraiser? You could send out a letter to all our friends and family sharing Henry's story and what we want to accomplish by sending him to Israel," I suggested.

Drew had another idea.

"What if I go to Israel with him, film the trip, and put a documentary together of his journey?" he suggested. "Then each donor can get a copy of it."

Oh, boy, I wasn't expecting this big of a project. But I knew this could be the answer to the question he had been searching for the last six months about his deeper purpose. I also knew that he was getting a God shot and needed to go with it.

"Okay," I agreed. "Let's reach out to Henry and see if he would be interested in our little plan."

The next evening, we gave Henry a call to tell him about our idea.

"Hello?" We heard Henry's voice, deep and deliberate, on the other end of the phone.

"Hi, Henry, this is Jen Principe, Drew's mom," I said.

"Yes, I know who you are. I recognize that lovely voice. How are you and what can I do for you, Jen?" he inquired.

"Well, Henry, Drew is here with me, and we would like to propose something to you."

"Oh?"

"Henry, we are very touched by your story. Drew has an idea we would like to share with you: he wants to send you to Israel. He would like to reunite you with your cousin and get you bar mitzvahed at the Western Wall. He would also like to contact Yad Vashem and have them change the paperwork showing that you are a living survivor of the Holocaust. To do this, he would like to organize a fundraiser in your honor. Is this something you would consider?"

There was a long pause as we waited for Henry's response.

"I am so touched, but this is just too much to accept," he finally said.

"Henry," I said, "Drew really wants to do this. And he would also like to come with you to Israel and document your journey."

"Well, I just don't think I could accept such a huge gift like this. Besides, I would not go without my wife, Susie."

"Okay. That's not a problem. We will raise enough money for the both of you," I responded.

"This is just too big. I am so touched by your generosity, but I will have to graciously decline."

"Henry, could you please just give this some thought?" I begged him.

"Yes. I will think about it and get back to you, my dear," he said.

Drew looked disappointed when I hung up the phone. I really wanted Henry to accept the trip too, but after hanging up, I wasn't sure he would.

The next morning, I called Henry privately, just to give it one more effort. I told him about Drew's desire to go into the military and his recent struggle to find some purpose and meaning in his life. I told him that by accepting this gesture, he might give Drew some depth and the purpose he was clearly searching for right now. Henry listened intently and asked if he could talk to his wife and get back to us.

That following evening, we got a phone call from Henry. He said that he would agree to accept the gift of a trip to Israel on the conditions that Susie would come with him and that there would be *no* bar mitzvah.

We were relieved and excited to hear that he had accepted our offer but shocked to hear about the bar mitzvah. When we questioned Henry about it, he told us that he had been offered a dozen or more times, but that he has never wanted one and, once again, he would have to decline our offer as well.

We were stunned. I thought, *How is Drew going to raise the money without this meaningful and one important tradition?* When I asked Henry if there was a reason, these were his exact words: "Because I don't believe in God after everything I have seen."

My heart dropped when I heard this. Yet I understood. I've grappled with the same issue before. *How could God allow such cruelty?* Henry lived it. Who am I to tell him, a Holocaust survivor, to believe in God, especially after everything he had witnessed in his life? I had absolutely no idea what it would feel like to be in Henry's shoes.

There was a long silence on the phone after Henry explained his position and that there would be no bar mitzvah. But then, I felt a sense of calm come over me, and I just knew that it didn't matter if he had a bar mitzvah or not—we were going to get Henry and Susie to Israel, regardless. And the words just fell from my mouth.

"Henry, I respect your decision and your belief. We are going to send you and Susie to Israel, regardless. But we do believe in God, and we believe that God speaks through people and that He is speaking through Drew," I said. "Thank you for accepting, and we are honored to be a part of this journey."

I hung up the phone, and Drew looked relieved but disappointed that Henry had declined to have this rite of passage in the Holy Land. But this was going to be Drew's mission trip, and we would not be joining him. He would be going with his brother and documenting this trip to, hopefully, find the answers he needed to the questions about life—with or without a bar mitzvah for Henry.

That week, Drew began drafting the letter that we would be sending out to our friends and family. Just before we were about to send them out, we received a phone call late one evening. It was Henry. I was nervous when I saw his name appear on my phone.

"Hello?" I answered.

"Hello, Jen," said the voice on the other end. It was Henry, sounding shaky and not at all like his normal tone.

"Yes, is everything okay, Henry?" I could hear him sniffling.

"I'm sorry to bother you this late, but I must tell you something," he said, his voice quivering.

"It's no problem, Henry. What's going on?" I asked nervously.

"I don't even know how to properly describe what happened to me. Last night, I had a dream about my father. I haven't seen him or dreamed about him in seventy-six years. My dream was that my father was trying to give me my bar mitzvah. The dream felt so real, like he was there. I woke up from my dream and immediately woke Susie up. I knew it was time. I said, 'It's time . . .' It's time for me to have my bar mitzvah."

Chills ran through my body, and I started to cry on the other end of the phone. I ran into Drew's room and woke him up to tell him the good news. When I told him, he looked at me and said, "It's a God shot, Mom."

Remember how I said to Drew that when you listen to your inner voice, it feels like everything flows toward you? Well, the river started flowing the minute we sent those letters out. We raised enough money to send Henry and Susie to Israel, all expenses paid, within just a few weeks.

We also called our friend and rabbi, Ron Li Paz, to see if he would be going to Israel anytime during the summer. He told us he had a trip planned in June with a group of adults to officiate bar/bat mitzvahs at the Western Wall. Hearing this couldn't feel more serendipitous; it was truly meant to be.

When we asked him if Henry and Susie could join the group, the rabbi replied that he would be so honored—he had never performed a bar mitzvah for a Holocaust survivor. Drew's letter circulated around our community and eventually even made international news. The publicity helped get the attention of Yad Vashem (the holocaust museum), a welcome change from the numerous requests to change Henry's paperwork—changing his status to reelect that he was, indeed, alive—that previously went ignored. Once the world news was involved, not only did the museum change the paperwork, but they also held a private ceremony at the museum recognizing Henry as a survivor during our visit.

Drew's letter also caught the attention of a local rabbi from another synagogue, Rabbi Shlomo, who then asked if he could meet Drew and Henry because he was so touched by the story that he began raising money at his own temple to support Drew's cause. What happened next seemed just short of a miracle.

Rabbi Shlomo came over to meet Henry and Drew and, while they were talking, the rabbi asked Henry if there was anything he could do for him while he was in Israel. Henry asked him to arrange a visit with the chief Orthodox rabbi of Israel, Rabbi Lau. Surprised by Henry's request, Rabbi Shlomo inquired for the purpose of this meeting. Incidentally, it turns out that Rabbi Lau and Henry were liberated together, and they hadn't seen each other in seventy-two years. For Rabbi Shlomo, this would not be an easy wish to fulfill since Rabbi Lau is one of the most prominent figures in Israel. Yet Rabbi Shlomo said that he would give it his best effort.

As the trip grew closer and Henry prepared for his bar mitzvah, we held a gathering at our home for all the donors to meet Henry, have them hear his story, and thank them for being a part of this experience. We decided that we wanted to get Henry a tallit, or prayer shawl, to be worn at his upcoming ceremony and to have his name inscribed on it in Hebrew. When I called him to ask if he had been given a Hebrew name, I couldn't believe my ears.

"Yes, my Hebrew name is Asher," he said.

I gasped. Drew's Hebrew name is Osher, which is, essentially, the same name, akin to an "Anthony" meeting a "Tony." This was just another sign that validated Henry and Drew's preordained soul connection.

Drew was named after my grandfather, Osher; the English translation of Asher or Osher means "happiness." Again, another one of the synchronistic moments surrounding Henry and Drew.

So, that night, just a few weeks prior to his upcoming trip, Henry told his story to our family and friends; there was not a dry eye in the room. After he told his story, we wrapped both Henry and Susie in their prayer shawls and recited the blessings with each person creating a circle that engulfed them. It was at that moment that I realized I needed to be there in Israel, to be a part of the incredible journey they were about to embark on. That night, my husband and I decided to book our tickets to be a part of this once-in-a-lifetime experience and celebration.

We decided we would join them halfway into their trip; the boys would have the first half to be alone with Henry and Susie. So, Drew and his brother Jeremy loaded their cameras and headed off on an adventure of a lifetime. When they landed in Tel Aviv, Drew arranged to have them taken to see Olga, Henry's cousin, for the first time. My sons watched through their camera lenses as the last two people of the same bloodline embraced for the very first time. I asked Drew what it was like to watch their union, and he said there are certain things that just need to be felt in order to explain them.

The next morning, they received an unexpected phone call. Security would be picking the four of them up and bringing them to meet Rabbi Lau, the chief Orthodox rabbi of Israel and Henry's long-lost friend. It turns out that Rabbi Shlomo pulled some strings and really felt compelled to make Henry's wish come true. Everyone dressed up in their suits and were escorted by security across town to meet the prominent Rabbi Lau.

When they entered the room, the rabbi was sitting behind his desk and waved them into the room. My son said he looked frail and much smaller than Henry. They introduced one another and shook hands with the rabbi, with the exception of Susie, since the ultra-Orthodox don't touch women. My son turned on the recorder and watched in awe as Rabbi Lau made the connection: that he and Henry shared a connection when Henry referred to him as "Luleg," his nickname in the concentration camp.

Rabbi Lau was one of the youngest survivors of the Holocaust and now understood who Henry was and why he came to see him. Henry was the first and only Holocaust survivor who had ever come to visit the rabbi. Once the connection was made, Henry handed him a copy of his book, *The Kindness of the Hangman*, while Rabbi Lau gifted his, entitled *Out of the Depths*. As they glanced through each other's books, they suddenly both stopped at a photo each of them had put into their books. In it, fifteen boys are huddled together, with Rabbi Lau at eight years old on one end, and Henry, at age seventeen, on the other. The photo was taken on April 15, 1945, the day they were liberated. Drew captured this powerful moment as Henry and Rabbi Lau pointed themselves out to each other.

Rabbi Lau turned to Henry and said, "I understand you are going to be having a bar mitzvah this week at the Kotel (Western Wall)."

Henry smiled and said, "Yes, I am. It's time."

The rabbi then asked Henry if he could perform a very ancient and religious practice that observant Jews do once they reach the age of thirteen, called "laying Tefillin."

Tefillin are special black boxes and leather straps placed on one's head and inner side of the left arm. The ritual is performed every morning, and its commandment literally means to bind oneself to the will of God. While this is something Henry said he would never do (after all, he didn't believe in God), in that moment, he had a change of heart. With the camera still rolling, Henry began rolling up his sleeves to expose the numbers forever inked on his forearm, identifying him as a prisoner of war. Rabbi Lau gently pointed and touched Henry's numbers and commented that he did not have the tattoo. Rabbi Lau then looked up at Henry and began ceremoniously wrapping his left arm with the black leather straps that so poignantly covered the numbers that lay underneath. Henry's eyes filled with tears, and his voice began to quiver as he recited each Hebrew word. Behind the lens, tears streamed down Drew's face as he watched these two Holocaust survivors perform this ritual. When I asked Drew to describe what it felt like, all he could say was that it was one of the most powerful and spiritual moments he will probably ever experience in his lifetime.

Henry had his bar mitzvah at the Western Wall, the most religious site in the world for the Jewish people. Drew stood by Henry's side as he tearily recited the blessings and completed the ritual that his father had so desperately tried to give him in the ghetto seventy-six years ago. I'm sure his father would have been very proud. Afterward, we all danced and sang and celebrated. Drew turned to me and said, "This is the best day of my life." It reminded me of a quote by Gretta Brooke Palmer: "Happiness is a by-product of an effort to make someone else happy."

On our last night in Israel, we were invited to a culmination dinner for the adults who had bar/bat mitzvahs. Each of them now shared a special bond and had formed an unforgettable and unique friendship with Henry and Susie. We had finally arrived at the apex of this journey, and when asked to share the most memorable part of the trip, each person mentioned Drew and how his act of kindness gave them the opportunity to be a part of Henry's journey and changed their lives too. Henry was the last person to speak. He stood up and turned to Drew.

He looked down at his bracelet and said, "I have spoken all over the world and to many schools. I have never once had a student approach me and give me anything, especially something that belonged to them. This bracelet that you have given me, I will never take off, and it is one of the most valuable gifts that I have ever received. What we have, Drew, is not friendship, it's kinship. You are like a grandson to me."

Then he reached into his pocket and pulled out a necklace with a circular medallion with an inscription on it, the Shema Y'srael, the same inscription etched into his leather bracelet. How apropos that the first word in the prayer is "hear," as in "to listen." Drew listened to his inner voice and to the God shot. He listened, and he found the will to move forward and take that first step. We all learned, through Drew and Henry, the importance of both giving and receiving. One little act of kindness can change so many lives, and the unexpected reward is that the helper reaps even greater benefits than the one helped. Henry placed the necklace around Drew's neck, and we all watched as they embraced one another. It occurred to me that Drew was the exact same age that Henry was when he was liberated. In some ways, then, they both became free at seventeen.

Drew was liberated from his fear of not finding his purpose. He learned that being of service was a way out of fear and into finding meaning in his life. He learned that one small act of kindness can change the trajectory of so many, and the powerful ripple effect that one person can create. I was proud, and I knew that Drew had found his purpose, at least for now.

Sadly, Henry passed that following year, but we think his life came full circle because of the unexpected friendship he had developed with Drew. In the end, we were able to help Henry find the missing puzzle pieces in the Holy Land. I know that Henry had alluded to the idea that there were miracles all around him when he was in Israel, but I don't think he ever came around to believing in a god. And while we do believe, we don't believe that this is necessary. We all have access to an inner voice, regardless of what we believe in, that urges us to listen.

Henry did, however, proudly wear his bracelet every day until his last days here on this earth, and although Drew didn't choose to go into the military, he wears the necklace Henry gave him like a badge of honor and has since tattooed a replica of the medallion on his arm. What was once considered an inexpensive souvenir has become a treasured family heirloom. One day, Drew will hand it down to his child or grandchild and, hopefully, it will be worn rather than stored in a box or tucked in the back of a closet somewhere. I, too, will give the Judith Leiber bag to my granddaughter or daughter-in-law and retell the story of how it had been gifted to me and purchased both on my birthday, November 24, twenty-one years apart.

As I was writing this book, I became curious about Judith Leiber's past. I did a little research and, to my surprise, I learned that Henry and she had something unbelievable in common. They were both Holocaust survivors. Before you toss out that gifted piece or heirloom that you think is out of fashion, let's rethink their significance and find a way to add them into your wardrobe.

If you are interested in seeing Drew's video on YouTube, simply scan the QR code below to watch his documentary. You can also purchase a copy of Henry's book, *The Kindness of the Hangman*, on Amazon.

CHAPTER 4

Letting Go and Letting In

"Clearing the clutter in your physical space will go a long way toward clearing the clutter in your mind and relationships."

—PETER WALSH

Purging your wardrobe is like having sex or going to the gym. Sometimes, you're super tired or you don't really feel like doing it, but when you do, you feel amazing, euphoric, and think, *Wow, I should do this every day.*

As a stylist, I've worked with a wide range of wardrobes, but it is so difficult for my creativity to flow when a closet is cluttered and disorganized. And, if it's hard for *me*, I can only imagine how frustrating it is for my clients. A cluttered closet is like a cluttered mind: if you have too much useless information, it's difficult to formulate what you are trying to say or accomplish.

When I first meet a new client, one of our tasks is to purge and let things go. At this point, I know some of you might want to close this book and say, "No, thank you." But don't worry. It's okay. I'm here to help, and trust me when I say I have no judgments about the state of your closet. I've seen it all!

Before beginning this exciting, new journey of fashion and raising your vibration through the power of clothes, we need to start by cleaning up your own mental closet and your own limiting beliefs so that we can be open, ready, and fearless as we move forward. Through my work, I have learned that sometimes people hold on to things out of fear—fear that they will need that one item one day in the future, whether it's for when they lose ten pounds or when they take that fantasy vacation that's yet to be booked. Sometimes we hold on to things because we are afraid we won't be able to afford to replace them when we need to or fear that, one day, we will regret having given them away.

All of these are limiting and untrue beliefs.

Clinging or attaching ourselves to these beliefs for a future moment that may or may not happen holds us back from being in the present and allowing the universe to work for us. As spiritual leader and healer Gabrielle Bernstein likes to say, we are "future tripping." That's when we get into our heads and create scenarios about a future that doesn't yet exist. In my world, I call it "mental closet clutter," where we are filling our heads with unnecessary thoughts and beliefs; it just takes up mental and physical space that keeps us trapped and cluttered. When we *closet clutter*, we are working at odds with the Law of Attraction. Relinquishing your unused, unwanted clothing and making space for the new allows the universe to work for us, as long as we trust in it.

Personally, I like to visualize the things that aren't serving me. This makes it easier to let things go. I imagine people walking around somewhere in this world wearing something that was once just taking up time and space in my own closet. I imagine them going about their lives in my colorful zigzag print Missoni sweater (that never quite fit me properly) or my four-and-a-half-inch patent leather Christian Louboutin Mary Janes (that look incredible but come with *significant* foot pain I'm no longer willing to endure) now bringing them joy, warmth, or comfort (metaphorically speaking). I also let go of the fear that, one day, I will regret giving it away because I believe that something better will manifest when I need it, at precisely the right time.

I have seen the power of the Law of Attraction work in my own life, in full force. In my seminars, "How to Be Your Own Personal Stylist," we go over one important step that I like to refer to as "style stalking," which is using social media as a platform for gleaning style inspiration. In my own phone, I have curated a collection of looks that inspire me and that I want to incorporate into my own wardrobe. One of the photos I had saved in my style-stalking folder was of a pink, patterned, one-shoulder ruffle top and skirt set that I had loved and admired for a very long time. It's bold and fashion-forward, exactly my vibe. I would look at the picture often and visualize myself wearing it. But I didn't know who the designer was or from where I could buy it, despite cleverly styling it for myself in my head already.

About a year later, I was prepping for a fast-approaching TV segment. I found myself so busy with my own clients and styling the models for the upcoming segment that I forgot about a charity event in which my husband and I were being honored that same evening. I didn't take the proper time to plan what *I* would be wearing in front of hundreds of guests. With every minute accounted for that week, I pulled out my phone and began quickly sifting through my lookbooks while waiting to go on air. For some reason, the phone defaulted to opening Instagram, and there it was, right before my eyes: my feed showed a picture of one of my best friends wearing what I thought looked incredibly similar to the two-piece outfit I had been coveting for over a year. It would be *perfect* for the grand opening. The color palette didn't look exact, and it was styled slightly differently but looked similar enough. I immediately rang up my girlfriend and asked if I could borrow her outfit and grab it on my way home from the studio.

"Of course you can!" she said, flattered I had asked to borrow it. When I went to pick it up, I was stunned. It was the *exact* outfit I had seen a year ago; the filter she had used on the picture had altered the pink hue in her photo. The Law of Attraction strikes again. I may not have been able to find the outfit while I was shopping and was obsessed about it for a year on my phone, but it's a great example of how the universe was working in my life—and the best part was, I didn't even have to spend a penny!

When I'm working for my clients and shopping for them, I also like to ask the universe to show me the perfect pieces to add to their life and their wardrobe. I ask to be of service to my client because it never hurts to ask, and the remarkable thing is the universe shows up and delivers every time it's supposed to.

I recently had this exact experience with one of my clients who had a very important red-carpet event that was quickly approaching, which I needed to find a dress for. I like to ask my clients prior to shopping for a special event what they visualize themselves wearing and what the perfect outfit looks like in their imagination. As she was describing her dream dress and vibe, I instantaneously knew what I was going to get for her. Just a few days prior to meeting with her, I was out shopping at one of my favorite department stores, Saks Fifth Avenue, and this stunning, forest-green, satin Veronica Beard dress just hit the floor. I remember thinking at the time, *I want to find a client for this amazing dress!* I also knew it was going to sell out ridiculously fast. So, while she was describing her fantasy fashion vibe, this immediately jogged my memory. I knew the cut would flatter her body perfectly because she was a little self-conscious of her midsection, and the dress had pleats and ruche in all the right areas. The design of the dress also had a dramatic shoulder pad, which would create the illusion of a smaller waist and a more hourglass shape.

I knew she would love this Veronica Beard dress and immediately called studio services to have it set aside for me. I could see it paired with the crystal dramatic chandelier Rosantica earrings I had sold to her previously, a gold single-strap Gianvito Rossi sandal, and a leopard-print clutch. Unfortunately, I was right—the dress was selling out fast. Saks had sold out her size, and I looked on every website; there was no size ten or twelve to be found. I called all my contacts to no avail. The satin dream dress was not available in her size. So, I decided to order the size fourteen as an option with the hopes of having it altered. Of course, I brought a few backup options that were beautiful, but in my mind, my heart was still set on the green goddess dress. When I got to her home for the fitting, I unzipped the hanging dress bag and when her eyes caught the green dress, she gasped at the sight of it.

"Oh my God! I love that," she said.

But before she got her hopes up, I regretfully had to tell her that her size was sold out and that I had to order it two sizes bigger than what she normally wears. She was still excited about the dress and tried it on first, but sadly, there was just too much excess delicate fabric to have it altered properly. We had to choose an alternative. The size ten would have been perfect!

During my long drive home, I listened to a podcast about the five simple rules of divine timing. I love this topic, and it's taken me a long time to develop an understanding about not getting attached to my own personal timelines and plans. Retrospection offers me the wisdom of relaxing a bit and trying not to force pieces that don't fit. Well, perfect timing was in alignment for my client because, when I got home, I hopped on the computer to work, only to receive an email notification from one of the websites for an automatic "back in stock" notification request. The dress was in stock, and I was able to order her the dress! And, just as I suspected, the size ten fit her perfectly.

Part of your fashion journey is learning to let go about letting go. I, like you probably, used to have a fear of letting go and purging my clothes. I have also had to let go of a lot of my beliefs to get to where I am today, which I'll discuss more in detail in the next chapter. If we let go in order to let *in*, then we shift the emphasis from giving up and the pain of releasing to the joy of receiving. In fact, this book is a perfect example of the universe working in both your life and mine. For whatever reason, the universe has put this in your hands so you can receive my wardrobe wisdom.

Deciding what to keep and what to let go of can be stressful and overwhelming. Before you begin decluttering your closet, make sure you allocate a sufficient amount of time toward the process. My suggestion is to work in sections and take breaks in between so you don't become overwhelmed and frustrated. A clothing rack to separate your clothes can also be very helpful. Plan to try on clothes during the process, so don't schedule this after an arduous sweaty workout. In fact, you should look and feel your best. Nothing looks good when you don't feel good about your appearance.

I have a few hard rules when decluttering:

1. Never let go of anything that has sentimental value to you.

2. Never toss anything that brings you pure joy. I don't care if it's not on trend. If it creates positive energy for you, then it should be kept and worn. It's up to you and a personal choice. Of course, that doesn't mean you keep all your keepsakes if you're ready to let go of them.

3. Don't keep clothes that are torn, stained, bleached, worn out, or don't fit you properly.

4. Don't keep anything that you have never liked; it won't grow on you.

5. If you're not sure about the cut or the fit because it's been sitting in your closet for too long, try it on and evaluate. Perhaps it needs

alterations. Pair down your wardrobe by looking at multiples and analyze your lifestyle. If you have five black dresses but gravitate toward your favorite two, then ask yourself why and when you would choose the other three dresses above your favorites. While you may have ten pairs of jeans, do you really need all those different choices? If you're not sure about the cut or the fit because it's been sitting in your closet for too long, try it on and evaluate.

If you haven't worn an item in twelve months, ask yourself why. You might find it doesn't fit your lifestyle any longer, you've never liked it to begin with, or you're simply afraid you might miss it and regret giving it away. If the latter is the case, then give it a timeout. Store it in a timeout box or some vacuum-sealed bags and date them. If you haven't pulled the items back out within twelve months, then consider donating them.

Now, let's dive into my guidelines when it comes to vintage (more on this in Chapter 5), classic pieces, and accessories.

What's Old Is New

When it comes to fashion, what goes around always comes back around eventually, usually in twenty-year cycles. So, it's no surprise that the current '90s trend of high-waisted mom jeans, fanny packs, mini-backpacks, crop tops, neon, shoulder pads, bike shorts, etc. are all over the runway. If we know trends will return, the question becomes, What should we hang on to? And: What are the best investments to buy for the future?

The two rules I follow regarding vintage items and whether you should keep or sell them are:

1. They must look good on your body type and fit well (unless you're saving for a family member); and

2. They must be in good condition (or can be repaired to look new again). If it doesn't fit into either of those two categories, then let it go, regardless of whether it's designer or high-end couture.

What to Keep

When it comes to vintage items, here are my dos and don'ts:

Family Heirlooms: DO keep these. Never get rid of a family heirloom or a sentimental gift, because family and love *never* go out of style. Try adding the vintage brooch your mother or grandmother gave you to your dress or blazer and think of her when pinning it onto your lapel. I wore a gifted brooch from my mother-in-law to my twenty-five-year wedding renewal, pinned to my white Ronny Kobo sheer dress. It looked perfectly stylish.

Bags: DO keep investment classics. Hermès, Chanel, and Dior are just a few classics and *will* hold their value. If they are well taken care of, they can also last a lifetime. The quilted Chanel 2.55 bag, born in 1955, the classic "The Lady" Dior bag from 1994, or a classic Tom Ford suit with a great pair of vintage Linda Farrow sunglasses will never ever go out of style.

Every designer comes out with an "It" bag or fashion trend for the season. These are usually good investments. For example, the Dior Saddle bag, born in 1999 and known for being tucked comfortably under the armpit with its famous kidney shape, made a huge comeback in 2021. If you can catch the trends as they are reemerging, you can pick up the vintage version, sometimes at a fraction of the cost at online stores, like The RealReal or What Goes Around Comes Around or eBay. And, in my opinion, having the original version is always more stylish than the newer one.

Different designers are hot at different times, so pay attention to when fashion houses change creative directors and designers. For example, Bottega Veneta is a classic, known for its Intrecciato basketweave, timeless elegance, and longevity. After the appointment of its new brand creative director, Daniel Lee, in 2018, the brand is now making a huge impression on the runway. The classic brand's twist on the new square-toe shoe and buttery, basketweave shoulder bags are one of the hottest trends today. But it's also a testament to the brand's timelessness: their iconic handbags have endured the test of time, and pulling one back out of your closet from decades ago or picking one up from a vintage store that may be from a few seasons ago can add some instant chic to your wardrobe.

Gucci also made a huge comeback when the brand appointed Alessandro Michele as its new creative director in 2015. The brand was already one of the most coveted out there, whether it was fashion lovers wanting to own a Gucci belt, an embellished tennis shoe, or a Gucci logo canvas or GG Marmont handbag. However, the logo and the brand's iconic symbols of the bee and horse have all stood the test of time—so hang on to those classics. When buying, try to stay away from anything too trendy; again, stick with the classics. I still have a pair of Gucci gold-strap sandals with the historic Gucci bee from twenty years ago that I wore during a fashion segment on Los Angeles TV station KTLA, and I still carry the very first designer bag—of course, Gucci—that my husband bought me in Paris twenty-five years ago. And if you don't follow trends, you can always follow me on Instagram for the latest tips and tutorials on who's hot and what's hot.

Clothing: When it comes to clothes, DON'T keep items just because they are designer or have a label. DO keep ones that are classic, timeless, or that make you feel special when you wear them, especially if they look good on you. Coats are usually keepers and rarely need to be updated or replaced, especially if you buy classic shapes and styles such as trench coats, classic wool coats, faux furs, bombers, and leather jackets.

Quality: When shopping for vintage clothes, DO recognize quality and details. Great fabrics and details can beget great clothes. Touch and feel. Stay away from microfibers that don't feel good to the touch. Look at the buttons, stitching, and seams. Seams should be straight and hems double stitched. Check for puckering and excess fabric. Check to make sure that the linings are sewn straight. Last, check zippers, as they should zip easily without excess puckering.

Shoes: Shoes can be tricky because they come back in style but usually with a slight twist. Unless you have the room to store your shoes for decades, here are my suggestions for what to keep: If it's a high-end designer classic like a Chanel flat, a Manolo Blahnik kitten heel, a Christian Louboutin classic pump, or a runway "It" shoe, like the 2010 edgy, luxe, rock-studded T-strap from Valentino or a Ferragamo square-heel closed toe—hang on to those! Pulling one of those out of your wardrobe in twenty years will have everyone coveting the original. However, most shoe trends reemerge with a slight variation to them. For example, the closed-toe pointy pump from the '80s and '90s had a *much* pointier toe and came higher up the ball of the foot, as opposed to the closed-toe pumps of the 2000s that were more rounded near the toe and partially exposed the toes, revealing what's known as "toe cleavage." So, DO hold on to classics and the "It" designer shoes if you have the room, and make sure you have a good shoe repair person whom you trust.

Accessories: I rarely get rid of my sunglasses, belts, hats, or statement jewelry pieces. Belts are unique and, in my opinion, rarely go out of style. I love a studded vintage or equestrian-style belt on a dress for unexpected fashion. A vintage pair of Ray-Bans or Linda Farrow sunglasses will always rock an outfit. A statement jewelry piece, especially one you found on vacation, can both raise your vibration and create a unique personal style. Try a chunky necklace with a T-shirt, jeans, and simple felt fedora.

Speaking of hats, I keep all of mine. I love and collect them. From my vintage denim Von Dutch baseball hat and my Dior veil cap to my Gladys Tamez Faye hat, it's my opinion that hats add an element of instant chic to an outfit and scream confidence, for both men and women. And because fashion comes in cycles, you know you can always make old things new again!

In the next tutorial, I will show you how to easily move through your wardrobe and create a keepsake/timeout box, a donation box, and a tailoring section. I'm so excited for you to dive in!

CHAPTER 5

Relax, It's Not a Tattoo

"You can't go back and change the beginning,
but you can start where you are and change the ending."

—C. S. Lewis

I sometimes refer to God as GOD, an acronym that stands for "Guider of Direction." The word *God* can make some people feel uncomfortable, and that's the last thing I want my readers to feel. So, instead of God, let's use the acronym GPS, like the GPS map, because that is essentially what my God does for me to navigate and guide my direction. It's perfectly apropos because, as anyone who knows me can attest, I'm not a good driver and have no sense of direction.

I've learned to depend on my life GPS guide because it knows better than me where I'm headed and the fastest and easiest route to get there. That doesn't mean I won't encounter traffic. I will, and I have. It also doesn't mean that the roads will be smooth. As you dive deeper into this book, you'll see it's been a very rough and bumpy ride. It simply means that my GPS knows the best roads for me to take to reach my destination and has led the way for me to see that trauma is not a destiny. In fact, quite the opposite. Of course, I've veered off many times, thinking I know an easier, faster way—only to find myself *completely* lost. The good news is I've learned that my GPS is loyal and dependable and all I need to do is ask and trust it. It's led me here to you.

I have the numbers 11:11 tattooed on the side of my rib cage. I put a lot of thought into having these symbolic numbers inked onto my body before making the commitment to permanently modify my torso. For me, this visual display is a personal and spiritual reminder to let go of fear and remember that my GPS map is in control. This wasn't always easy for me, considering I had very little control over my childhood and lived in a constant state of fear.

I never knew when Tia would have a fit of rage and lash out at me with her fists. The smallest of incidents would set her off. I have a vivid memory of her storming into my room the day before my thirteenth birthday, grabbing me by the hair, and throwing me to the floor.

"Pick up this damn shit, you dirty slob," she sneered.

I grabbed my clothes, which included a pair of my underwear where my menses had leaked through the sanitary pad, leaving a stain. She grabbed my hair again, pulling me to my feet. Then she grabbed me by the ear and shoved me down the stairs as she repeatedly slurred the words "niña sucia" ("dirty girl" in Spanish). My ears turned bright red and hot. By the time we reached the washing machine, I was crying, repeatedly saying I'm sorry. She slapped me hard across the face; my cheeks stung, and the blood quickly rushed to my face.

"How many times have I told you to pick up your underwear? You are disgusting and dirty. Just look at your underwear," she growled.

I looked down at the pair of underwear, stained with blood. An innocent girl's mistake. I looked up into her eyes, with tears in my own, and felt ashamed, embarrassed, and scared all at once.

She then said, "Smell them." I knew I would be in serious trouble, as there was no way I would do that.

"No, Mama. I'm sorry, I don't want to smell them. Please, I'll wash them, I promise," I begged.

Then came the first slap.

"Smell them!" she demanded. I could smell the alcohol still lingering on her breath from the night before. "I want to teach you a lesson. No man will ever want you if you are dirty!"

"No, Mama, please stop."

Another slap.

The force of my sobs made it hard for me to breathe. By the fourth slap, her nail caught the corner of my eye socket, carving a gash right underneath my eye. The sting of the wound—I can still feel it today—caused me to instinctively raise my fist, punching her as hard as I could. Tia fell backward, hitting her back on the counter directly behind her, and gasped in complete shock. I was ready to hit her again and defend myself if I had to, something she must have sensed, because she didn't strike me back. Instead, she walked away. And that was the last time I can remember Tia ever hitting me.

Sadly, though, the verbal abuse continued, and her drinking escalated to an entirely new level. She had lost some of her control over me, and although we had moments when we would get along, our relationship was never the same. When I was seventeen years old, things got so ugly between us that trading verbal insults with each other became a daily routine. That is, until Elisa, the new nineteen-year-old housekeeper arrived, and Tia began tormenting her instead. Elisa was 5'5" and about one hundred pounds, with long, naturally wavy thick hair, a perfect perky ass, and size D (real) boobs.

You're probably wondering, *What does this have to do with clothes and fashion?* That traumatic episode at the washing machine and so many others during my childhood began a series of beliefs I held about myself. Years of mental file folders filled with old beliefs, including: "I'm not good enough," "Everyone will betray me," "Everyone lies," "People don't want to help me," "I'm not special," "I will get hurt," "I can't trust anyone," "Everyone will steal from me," and "I am dirty."

I also knew that the "I'm not good enough" belief was holding me back in my styling career. When I first got into the business, I reached out to Elyse Walker for advice. Elyse is the founder of one of the biggest retail sites, Forward by Elyse, and owns several of the most successful fashion boutiques in Southern California. She works with some of the biggest A-list entertainers in the world, and her store is always filled with actors, stylists, and some of the most coveted runway clothes in the world. I didn't know Elyse personally but figured I would go to the best and see if she would *pay it forward*—and she did. Elyse was incredible and also intimidating.

Despite all her success, she was humble, kind, and extremely generous with her time. She was confident, forthcoming, and willing to answer all my questions. But after spending about an hour with Elyse, I left her store feeling more deflated than when I had gone in. I called my husband on the phone, and the first words out of my mouth were, "I can't do this. I'm not good enough!" to which he replied, "Jen, get out of your own way!" He reminded me that, before a big leap of faith, there's always a moment of doubt and I had to trust my GPS to guide me.

When you walk around with these negative stories about yourself, it makes it virtually impossible to succeed. One of my objectives in this book is to raise your vibration through clothes so we can transform you from the outside in. However, your insides and your outsides should match, meta-phorically speaking, and vice versa.

We are the creators of our own reality, a message we have been hearing so much in the last decade from books like *The Secret* and thought leaders like Esther (Abraham) Hicks, Dr. Wayne Dyer, and Gabrielle Bernstein. But this concept precedes all of them and can be traced as far back as Siddhartha Gautama (the Buddha). This isn't just about spiritual teachings; it's *wiring*.

The Reticular Activating System (RAS) is the short two-inch pencil-size piece of the brain located where it attaches to the spinal cord. It acts as the gatekeeper of information between most sensory systems and the conscious mind. It's like the bouncer of a night club, deciding who can gain entry. The brain is fed *so* much information that the RAS filters out unnecessary infor-mation. Contrarily, it also seeks information to support, justify, and validate your beliefs. It filters the world through the parameters that you give it, and your beliefs shape those parameters.

Let me say that again: *your beliefs shape your parameters*.

Some people believe that focusing your intent consciously on what you care about most and aligning your belief system with that conscious desire will present itself because your mind will tune in to the *right* information, helping you to find or achieve your goals. Meaning, you will always find the evidence for what you choose to believe. Sounds a lot like the Law of Attraction, right? It reminds me of a Buddhist saying: "All that we are is the result of what we have thought."

I have friends who are looking for love and constantly complaining that there are no good men out there. So, they keep meeting men that support this belief. When it comes to fashion, I have clients who tell me, "I could never wear that," or "I hate shopping," or "I'm terrible at dressing myself," or "I never find anything that looks good on me." They lament that they're too fat, not sexy, have no style, or refuse to take fashion risks. These untrue beliefs deprive them of experiencing the joy that comes with clothes and fashion and only push them toward experiences that align with their negative thoughts.

Thankfully, there are easy ways to become realigned. Have you ever wondered why, when you need to find the perfect dress, you can't find what you are looking for or feel like nothing looks good on you? While not everyone is privy to stylist secrets, that shouldn't prevent you from aligning yourself with someone who is. Which is why I'm so happy you picked up this book! It means you're ready to make a change in your thinking.

My mother-in-law is a perfect RAS master. When she was ready to meet her perfect match at the age of sixty, she began talking about him, detailing *everything* she was looking for. She wanted someone who was close to his faith, philanthropic, financially secure, adventurous, and willing to travel. It was important to her that he love and embrace her family and, of course, he must love animals. She even went as far as creating a vision board with the home she wanted to build together, places they could travel to, and even the dog she wanted. Within a short time—you guessed it—she found him.

Visualizing what you want is one thing; clearing the space to *receive* it is another. Now that we have *physically* cleaned out your closet and purged some of your wardrobe, the next step is to clean up your *mental* closet about your fashion beliefs and let go of any fear that may be holding you back. It's time to let your RAS work its magic.

But how, exactly, do we do that?

I've talked about divine timing, a concept I've seen play out so many times in my own life. When I was beginning my fashion career as a personal stylist, I constantly wondered why I wasn't feeling confident about my abilities to succeed. I mean, how could I with all those negative beliefs cluttering my mind? I decided to do something I had never done before: participate in an eight-day detox cleanse in Palm Springs, where I had my first experience with cleaning out my "mental filing cabinet."

The physical cleanse itself consisted of detox drinks that contained psyllium husk, one cup of vegetable juice, and one cup of very basic, very bland soup, plus tons of water. Every day, there was a variety of workshops and classes offered, like yoga, meditation, and breathwork. There was also a variety of treatments to support the body in detoxifying, like lymphatic massages, infrared sauna, endermology, mineral baths, and castor oil packs; I did all of them. The treatments helped take my mind off not having any solid food for one week. I had no idea that cleansing my body of toxins would be one of the most physically and mentally challenging things I've ever done, but it was well worth it.

Toward the end of the detox cleanse, my mind was clearer than I've ever experienced and I opened myself up to the prospect of doing even deeper work. Someone suggested that I do hypnosis with one of the therapists. So, on the last day, I took her advice and booked a session. I had no idea I was about to embark on a journey that would help change my belief system and, ultimately, my life. Now I would like to share this practice with you.

After making my appointment, I distinctly remember when my hypnotist arrived at my room. I took an immediate inventory of her. I was actively judging her book by its cover, and she seemed to fit the bill perfectly, smelling of essential oils and wearing a long flowing skirt with a bohemian-style blouse, layered with beaded Mala necklaces, one of which had a large crystal on it. Her demeanor was calm, assuring, and kind. I was feeling apprehensive and skeptical because I had never done anything like this before. But I also felt I had nothing to lose. In fact, it felt like the perfect time, as I was just beginning my styling career and swimming in a small ocean of self-doubt and fear. Maura had me sit across from her in a reclining chair and asked me to tell her about myself. So, naturally, I started from the beginning.

As if on autopilot, I told her my entire story, starting with my abandonment at six months old and ending with my dream job at age forty. I took a deep breath and waited for her instructions.

She smiled and said, "Well, you've come a long way, haven't you?"

Then we talked for a while about my limiting beliefs, which had transpired because of the trauma I had endured and was still holding on to. She paused a beat and asked, "Are you ready to let go of your story?"

"Yes, I'm ready," I replied, although I had no idea what would happen next or how it would even be possible to do this.

She relaxed me into a guided meditation. She told me to visualize a file cabinet with handles on both ends; inside the cabinet were folders. Each folder represented different chapters, memories, and beliefs from my life. She instructed me to visualize each year of my life and separate them into folders, putting them into the file cabinet in any order I chose.

After I was finished creating my mental filing folders, from childhood to adulthood, Maura asked me to make two more separate file folders to place at the back of the file cabinet. One was filled with positive beliefs that I believed about myself: I'm a hard worker, I'm creative, I'm a healer, I'm a helper, and I'm a good wife, mother, and a loyal friend. She told me to envision another folder directly behind it filled with all the negative beliefs about myself that we had discussed.

The file cabinet could be as big or as little as my imagination wanted it to be, and once all the folders were in the cabinet in their right order, the real work would begin. I was instructed to picture myself in a peaceful environment that she referred to as my "happy place." I imagined myself in a field of gardenias, like the ones my father used to leave in a bowl of water at my bedside. She asked me to bring the file cabinet to my happy place. Again, it could be as big or as little as I wanted it to be. She then asked me to tell her where it was in relation to me.

"Twenty feet away," I replied.

She told me to visualize myself walking over to the memory cabinet and reading the first file upon opening it. As I envisioned opening it, I saw that my memories were arranged in chronological order, starting from birth. I could see their labels clearly: Folder #1, Folder #2, etc.

She directed me to the very back of the cabinet and told me to pull out the last file, the one filled with negative beliefs, and to ask myself these questions: *Is the belief true, and how do I know for sure? If it was true then, is it still true now? And, last, is it serving me?*

"If the thoughts are untrue," she said, "I want you to visualize yourself destroying each of them one by one. You can tear them up, they can float away, you can burn them, you can use any method you like to permanently extricate them from your mind."

I went with the third option and imagined myself burning the folder, the ashes blowing away with a big gust of wind. She then asked me to visualize myself back in my peaceful place, sitting again, breathing and taking in the smell of my surroundings. I was to imagine the file cabinet rising from the floor from ten feet away from me and floating as far away in the distance so I could just barely see it across my field of gardenias.

"Before you set the cabinet down, I want you to rotate the cabinet completely so the very last folder is now in the front," she instructed. "So that if you ever need to go back into your past, it will start with the folder with all the positive beliefs you know to be true about you."

I finally understood why she had me put that folder at the very back of the cabinet.

"The next folders will begin with your amazing life *now*. The job that you love, your beautiful marriage and loving husband, your wonderful sons, your deep friendships, and so forth. There's no need to go all the way back into the cabinet and into your past because where you are headed is so much more important than where you have been," she said.

What she said reminded me of a quote I have always loved: "There's a reason why the rearview mirror is so small, and the windshield is so big: Because where you're headed is much more important than where you have been."

Like I said before, anyone who knows me well knows how appropriate this is because I'm really not the best driver and always need to keep my eyes forward! But, in all seriousness, those old files and unhelpful beliefs needed to go. I remembered how Elyse paid it forward and how thankful I am today that she did. I've had many calls from girls wanting me to pay it forward too and, because of Elyse, I always do. There's a seat in the house for everyone. If I had continued to believe those things about myself, I wouldn't have had the confidence to build a successful styling career. Envisioning my mental file cabinet and practicing this "purge" is a practice I still use today.

So, now that we have cleared out your closet and eliminated the things that were out of style or no longer serving you, we've made the physical and mental space for all the new things that are coming. The next vital step is to clean out your mental closet and challenge your fashion beliefs—as well as any others—that may be holding you back. Letting go of the fear around fashion is a huge step in allowing yourself to enjoy the process of moving outside of your comfort zone and embracing all the different benefits that dressing up can offer. There is sufficient evidence and psychological proof that clothes, colors, and fashion can elevate your mood and change your behavior, which I will discuss in the following chapter.

Without even a single word uttered, what we wear can speak volumes. And, whether consciously or subconsciously, we know this. There are two universal fears I find when it comes to fashion: 1) fear of being judged and 2) fear of making a fashion mistake. I will assure you that both will happen, and you'll be okay. I still make fashion faux pas, and people judge me all the time. But unlike me, you might not have to go as far as getting a permanent tattoo to remind yourself to *let go* of fear. On the contrary, fashion is anything but permanent, and sometimes, just knowing and remembering this can give you enough courage to go outside of your comfort zone. You can literally commit to wearing something outside your box for just one eight-hour workday. I have my own fashion motto I like to use with my clients when they feel intimidated or are afraid to wear something that's more fashion-forward than what they're used to: "It's not a tattoo. You can change it at any time." And take it from someone who actually *has* a tattoo!

This can help put someone at ease and be more open to experimenting with their wardrobe. Still afraid to make the big, fashion-forward jump? Well, you can start small. There are easy ways to begin expanding your style. Try painting your nails a different color, wearing a bright-hued lipstick, tying a patterned scarf to your bag, wearing a pair of brightly colored shoes, parting your hair to the other side, putting on a statement necklace, or donning a cool hat.

Don't get me wrong: there's still value in keeping a wardrobe classic and simple. I can absolutely curate a limitless array of wardrobe looks that are timeless and fashionable with the basics, as I described in the first chapter. But if you want a little more fun and excitement in your fashion life, you will have to embrace all that fashion has to offer you. Psychological research shows that fashion, as well as certain colors, can elevate your mood and change your vibration—almost instantaneously. So, the next time you go shopping, try raising your vibration from the get-go. Repeat some mantras to yourself, such as:

- "I'm going to find the perfect outfit for the occasion."
- "I will find the right person to guide me and show me what looks best on me."
- "I enjoy the process of shopping more today than I did in the past."
- "I will let go and try something different."

And the next time you start hearing those doubts start to creep in, such as, "I love that look, but I could never pull that off," remember it's *not* a tattoo.

Letting go can be an overwhelming task, both physically and mentally. So, bravo for creating space for both. Doesn't it feel liberating to walk into your closet now with less clutter? You're ready to download the free "Style-list" (get it!?) and take inventory of the items you're missing or need to replace. The next time you go shopping, you'll have your own personal Style-list guiding you and streamlining your mission, both in time and budget. Watch the next tutorial as I show you how it's done. Let's do this!

VIDEO TUTORIALS

CHAPTER 6

Garanimals

"Be weird, be random, be who you are.
Because you will never know who could love the person you hide."

—C. S. Lewis

My middle brother, Matthew, who is four years older than I am, is a mathematical savant. I remember hearing words floating around the house like, "mathematical genius," "photographic memory," and, perhaps more politically incorrect, "Rain Man" used to describe him. And while he was in possession of a unique, high-functioning brain, he lacked the social skills that, incidentally, came very easily to me (unlike math).

Matthew attended a school for gifted students for part of his elementary school years, but when he reached junior high, he began noticing and feeling like he didn't fit in. He had a much harder time making friends than I did, and his social circle was very small. Although I suffered a bit from anxiety and depression, I hid it well. I was invited to all the "cool" parties and social events. My idea of fun when I was in high school was to hang at Malibu Beach with my friends and listen to music with a group of good-looking surfers, all while working on my golden tan. His idea of fun was to travel long distances to get the highest score on the video game *Defender*. Our interests were diametrically opposed and, for the most part, we didn't understand each other at all. He hated fashion; I hated math.

By middle school, my brother struggled to make friends and had become something of a loner. Being in a larger public school environment, he felt different and was ostracized, which broke my heart. My brother would be the first to admit he had zero fashion sense and didn't really care about what he wore. He had no idea how to match colors, patterns, or styles and he didn't take any particular interest in learning how. Frankly, he just didn't care. Sometimes he would leave the house wearing a plaid shirt with striped pants that were clearly too short on him. His hair was never combed, let alone *styled*, and he wore thick-rimmed "nerd" glasses. This, sadly, made him the perfect target to be both teased and ignored.

Growing up with a workaholic father and without a proper mother figure, I became the bossy mother hen of the house. Intrinsically, I knew at a very young age that kids can be cruel and that what you wear can make a difference in how they treat you. So, when I was in fifth grade, and my brother in tenth, I decided to "Garanimals" his closet.

Garanimals was a line of children's clothing separates founded by Seymour Lichtenstein in 1972. The line featured hang tags depicting one of several animal characters used to teach children how to mix and match colors and patterns at an early age, simply by matching the animals. Being a parent, we all know the struggle of trying to get our little ones dressed in the morning, and sometimes, letting your child dress themselves can be disastrous. Convincing a child not to wear a ballerina tutu with cowboy boots to school on a snowy morning in the middle of January can be a real struggle. Lichtenstein's foolproof method was a win-win for both parent and child. It gave the child a sense of autonomy and confidence. I personally regard him as a brilliant man who combined the power of clothing and psychology to help children feel independent.

The struggle of trying to match wasn't unique to my brother by any means and, in my opinion, Lichtenstein is kind of a genius for figuring that out so early on. So, I did my own version of Garanimals for my brother. I color-coded his white plastic hangers with stickers and told him that he could only wear clothes that had matching color dots on the hangers: red with red, blue with blue, green with green, etc. And this all worked for a bit until he had to rehang things.

This temporary experiment, though, yielded some very valuable lessons that I believe to be true in my styling career today. One is that Matthew didn't hate clothes; he just didn't understand how to put them together, a clear example of "contempt prior to investigation." He had concluded about the fashion without having all the facts. Also, I learned early on—as a fifth grader—that clothes can almost immediately help us to feel more confident. I watched my brother match the dots, look in the mirror, and, literally, stand a half-inch taller. He carried himself differently altogether, with his shoulders pulled back, his chin lifted, and walked with a little more confidence. My brother, who couldn't care less about clothes and had even ridiculed me for "putting value on something so unimportant," was clearly enjoying his newfound swagger.

He looked at me, smiled, and said, "I really look good, don't I?" Like most people, once they learn how to do something, they tend to enjoy it more. Shortly after I "Garanimaled" his closet, he told me about his plans to ask out a girl who was in one of his AP classes to go roller-skating. He had never asked out a girl before, so we were both nervous. I think he knew he was going to need a little extra wardrobe help to give him a boost of confidence. In addition to picking out the appropriate color-coded hangers for the next day, we practiced his skating skills in the driveway for hours because you could never be too prepared.

The next day, he was nervous as he grabbed the outfit we picked out together: his burgundy OP surf T-shirt, straight-leg 501 jeans, a beige *Members Only* jacket, his white K-Swiss sneakers, and his Ray-Ban shades. Matthew looked in the mirror and smiled.

"What do you think?" he asked.

"Yes," I reassured him, the way a twelve-year-old younger sister would to the older brother whom she adored. Again, he looked a full half-inch taller with his shoulders back and his head held higher. As a result of my young styling prowess, my brother was beaming. Off to school he went with more self-assurance than I had ever seen him with. As I watched him pull away, I pictured him blaring cool music vibes through the parking lot and capturing all the attention of his peers as he confidently stepped out of his '65 Mustang Fastback with his new fashion sense. In my mind, everyone would "ooh" and "aww" over him in wonder. "Who is this cool kid?" they would ask. "Where did he come from?"

I continued fantasizing that, during lunch, he would see his crush across the tables in the quad and that their eyes would meet. Her heart would flutter as she noticed his studly new vibe. He would approach her with confidence and swag, sliding in next to her as he whispered in her ear, "You and me, Skating Plus, Friday night."

He was so confident that he didn't even have to ask her; he would *tell* her. And she would excitedly reply, "Finally! I've been hoping you would ask me out."

What can I say? I was twelve and had a wild imagination. I couldn't wait for him to come home and give me all the details of his day. But as it turns out, I'm a better stylist than a psychic. I would love to say that his newfound confidence (and his new personal stylist) earned him a date to the skating rink, but she turned him down. I guess a fifth-grade stylist can't solve all your problems. But, wow, did he look good that day.

Today, my brother is an accomplished anesthesiologist and well loved by his peers and family. He doesn't need fast cars or fancy clothes to get anyone's attention, but he understands the impact and value behind clothing and enjoys dressing up. While not nearly as awkward as he was in his preteens, he still doesn't fit in perfectly. It's one of the things I love about him most: he's perfectly imperfect. He still sometimes struggles with figuring out what to wear. Occasionally, I'll get a picture from him asking if his outfit matches, and I always smile and laugh. My brother, my very first client, showed me how I could empower others to feel good about themselves, and I have him to thank for launching what would become my career—all at the ripe old age of twelve.

So, today, Matthew still marches to the beat of his own drum. And so do I. *We all do.* And if that girl could see him today, she would be kicking herself for not doing the "hokey-pokey" with him.

Working with my brother also showed me the power of colors when it comes to clothes. At one point, I even wondered if my brother was colorblind because he had no concept of how to coordinate different tones. As I developed my career as a stylist, though, I realized, like a lot of people, he could identify colors perfectly; he just didn't understand which colors blended well together. He thus mostly defaulted to drab color shades or, when he *did* try something colorful, he would completely miss the mark. Which is a shame because colors have some powerful vibes! Did you know that colors have an energy to them and that some radiate at a higher frequency than others? Color plays a major role in our lives because of the way it influences our moods and emotions.

One of the easiest ways to immediately change and raise your vibration is through the use of color, as the colors you choose to wear correlate with how others perceive and respond to you. I realized this more than ever during the COVID-19 pandemic. During lockdown, it became very easy for me to fall into a wardrobe rut and stay in my black and gray sweats, or in my favorite Lululemon workout wear. But occasionally, for no apparent reason other than my psyche needed a little pick-me-up, I would dress myself in a bright-yellow Ganni wrap dress and a pair of fun Golden Goose sneakers and head off to the grocery store. I felt an immediate shift in energy, and I definitely had more bounce in my step. And what was even more amazing was how other people responded: I noticed they were so much more engaging and smiled at me more. I had several people comment to me that it was refreshing to see someone dressed up during these challenging times. I especially noticed the elderly responding to my colorful vibes. It made them feel happy. Even Gloria, the checkout lady at my local grocery store, who rarely ever says anything to me, was more loquacious than ever before, complimenting my bright attire.

I'm always intrigued when I meet someone who avoids wearing color; someone whose wardrobe consists of black, gray, and *maybe* a blue jean. But I'm a big believer that the choice between wearing or avoiding color can reveal something about one's personality. While wearing all black is chic, wearing it all the time, in my opinion, is just plain *boring*. And life's too short to be boring.

There are a few reasons why I think some people default to wearing all black. First, it's easy and takes the guesswork out of dressing. Steve Jobs was famous for his uniform of a black Issey Miyake turtleneck and blue jeans as he believed in the concept of "decision fatigue," the idea that we only have a finite capacity to make excellent decisions. In other words, the process of getting dressed was stressful and required too much brain power when it could be reserved for other things. Jobs preferred to save his decision-making capabilities for things that really mattered to him and wore black every day in order not to waste any time. Now, we can all agree that Steve Jobs didn't need to wear anything more "powerful" or that his clothing choices would have affected his business life any differently, but I would be curious if it would have affected his emotional life and shifted his energy.

I think another reason people choose to wear all black or gray is because they are slimming colors and, therefore, safe. Black is characterized by the absence of light, but because I, both literally and figuratively, want to bring as much light into every situation as possible, I feel like it's my personal mission to get my clients to incorporate some color into their lives.

Color plays a major role in our lives because of the way it influences our moods and emotions, so much so that it can trigger a negative response too. I once had a therapist relay a story about a girl who was adopted at the age of three. When she was ten years old, she had regressed, began urinating in bed, and refused to use her own bathroom. This went on for some time, until one day the mother found an old photo of her adopted daughter sitting in a crib in the orphanage and noticed that the walls were painted yellow. Suddenly she realized that she had just painted her daughter's bathroom the same color and brought the photo into the therapist's office to see if there was any correlation. The therapist confirmed the color yellow was triggering a negative memory and, therefore, retraumatizing her daughter. Once the walls were repainted, the problem resolved itself immediately. The power of color can't be underestimated.

On the contrary, one of the easiest ways to immediately change and raise your vibration is through color. The colors you choose to wear can correlate with how others perceive and respond to you. Certain colors can make you appear more confident, more approachable, and even more authoritative.

Still not convinced? You're not alone. I've heard a wide range of excuses from people about why their wardrobes are devoid of color: "Color doesn't look good on me," "I don't want to stand out," and "I'm not sure what colors to wear."

But here's the thing: color looks good on everyone! It's simply about finding the right colors that work for *you* and learning how to incorporate them into your wardrobe. Not wanting to stand out is a manifestation of fear, a topic we'll address in the next few chapters.

Decades of research support the psychology of color and how it can affect your mood, performance, and stress levels. Think of it in terms of weather: when it's been gray outside for a few days and the sun suddenly peeks out, it's an instant mood elevator, right? Colors send messages without being overt. Companies are keen to this information and choose to represent themselves using specific colors to convey certain images to the consumer. The color blue, often associated with the sky or the ocean, translates into stability, calmness, trust, and power. In fact, blue tops the list of *most used color* in Fortune 500 logos for this exact reason. It's also a great color for a person to wear on a first date or to negotiate an important business deal.

Red is the color of passion and implies excitement and gets the blood pumping, making it a great choice for a first date, especially for a woman. *The Journal of Personality and Social Psychology* published a study where men were shown side-by-side pictures of the same woman with two different backgrounds.[1] One background was white, and the other was red. The majority of the men found the woman pictured against the red background more desirable. Red is also perceived as direct, self-assured, and powerful. So, if you want to boost your confidence, invest in red. If wearing head-to-toe red is too daunting, start small: add in a bold red bag, a classic red lipstick, a closed-toe oxford red pump, or a bright-red scarf. See how this makes you feel and observe how others respond to you.

The same goes for other colors. Purple is often associated with luxury, wealth, and "the good life," so adding some purple into your wardrobe and pairing it with a neutral, like gray, conveys a message of grandeur. Green is the color of healing, success, and hope. White is associated with being trust-worthy, honest, pure, and perfect, which is why so many clergy wear it. Pink is the color of being playful and lighthearted and, unsurprisingly, one of the few colors missing from Fortune 500 companies. And, thankfully, variations within bold colors means you have plenty to choose from; if "millennial pink" isn't your thing, try a more mature magenta.

---

1 University of Rochester, "Psychological Study Reveals That Red Enhances Men's Attraction to Women," October 8, 2008, rochester.edu/news/show.php?id=3268.

Which brings us back to basic black. Black, although slimming, powerful, and professional, is also associated with aggression. A study of 52,000 National Hockey League games found that teams who wore all-black jerseys were penalized more for aggressive play.[2] So black, while basic and reliable, might not be conveying the message you want to send the rest of the world.

The fashion industry has been privy to the power of color to convey a message for decades now, through color and trend forecasting. But who comes up with the color trends for the seasons and the trendsetting runways? And how is it that different designers all stay within the same color palette for an entire season? Well, it has to do with a little company (and I'm being facetious here) known as Pantone. Pantone is a proprietary company that helped solve a common problem faced by many different industries, from tech to fashion: how to match and communicate colors across industries. The Pantone Matching System contains 1,925 different colors, each with a unique identifying number; the collection is the largest of its kind in the world, according to Laurie Pressman, Pantone's vice president of fashion, home, and interiors.

This system gives clarity and avoids mistakes across the supply chain so that canary yellow doesn't get mistaken for its sister color, dandelion. But Pantone is more than just the leader in color matching; they are also responsible for setting the fashion color trends for the year and have a hand in influencing the shades of roughly half of all garments sold in the US, according to NPD, a market research group.[3]

Picking these incredibly influential colors is like asking to be part of a top-secret, undercover mission. Pantone meets twice a year to choose their colors and the color of the year. A group of ten influential guests from a broad swath of industries are invited to serve on the committee. The names of these carefully selected individuals are kept secret, and the group meets in an all-white room so that everyone can see the objects being shown for

---

2 Larry Brown, "Study: Hockey Players Are More Aggressive When Wearing Black Sweaters," Larry Brown Sports, September 28, 2011, larrybrownsports.com/hockey/study-hockey -players-are-more-aggressive-when-wearing-black-sweaters/89337.
3 NPR, "The Business Of Color: Company Sets Fashion Trends," February 10, 2011, npr.org/2011/02/10/133636541/the-business-of-color-company-sets-fashion-trends.

inspiration as clearly as possible. Once again, psychology plays a role in determining the color of the year, a hue that ultimately translates onto the runway (among other places).

For 2021, Pantone chose Illuminating Yellow and Ultimate Gray as its colors of the year, signifying a light at the end of the tunnel of the COVID-19 pandemic. The colors are a reflection of the time we live in: gray being a solid and somewhat bleak hue, while yellow represents hopefulness and light. It's a more realistic palette compared to the calm Classic Blue color chosen for 2020, a year that turned out to be anything but. Once the colors are announced, their impact is almost immediate across all industries.

I'm always excited to see the seasonal colors fill the department stores and boutiques. If the color scheme doesn't work well with your skin tone, remember that there are many variations within that particular color palette. For example, if banana yellow isn't your hue, try a burnished gold instead.

As I alluded to before, color can be intimidating. I understand that. So, if neutrals are still your go-to, an easy way to add some color is by pairing a bright lip color, painting your nails a bright red, orange, or daring blue with a neutral all-black or all-gray outfit. Vivid lip colors instantly brighten a face and complexion. Color might seem intimidating—*but it doesn't have to be.*

Let's add some color to the time-capsule basics from Chapter 1 in the next tutorial and download the foolproof color-combining PDF. We'll also explore some basic visual rules for combining colors and what colors work with your skin tone, while adding some brightness and lightness to your world.

CHAPTER 7

Style Stalking and Finding Your Own Style

"If you want to be original, be prepared to be copied."

—Coco Chanel

When I was younger, I was a chameleon. Getting kicked out of school twice and attending four different high schools required me to acclimate to my changing surroundings and friends. I didn't want to stand out, so I did whatever I could to blend in, just like a chameleon would. Truthfully, like almost all teenagers, I didn't have any clue of who I was back in high school. I guess you could say being raised in an erratic, dysfunctional, and unstable environment has had a silver lining in that I was able to adapt easily to change. When I broke up with my first "real boyfriend," I was devastated, and my father once again came to the rescue, using clothes to communicate his concern and love to soothe my heartache. I came home to find a gray V-neck T-shirt lying across my bed that said, "Change is the law of life, and those that only look to the past or present are certain to miss the future," a quote I would later learn was from John F. Kennedy. Through that shirt, I learned the power of clothes can evoke particular emotions, a topic I'll be diving into deeper in the next chapter.

When I wore that shirt, I felt empowered and smart, because in reality, I didn't really feel either of those. I wore that shirt often. A statement T-shirt can have tremendous influence on both the wearer and the viewer because you are declaring some facet of yourself and portraying a message without the use of verbal communication. The famous "We Can Do It!" T-shirt of

Rosie the Riveter flexing her bicep, advocating for women's rights, became one of the most iconic T-shirts of all time for a reason. A statement tee can help create a mindset and an attitude to share with the world.

Today, when I see that quote by John F. Kennedy, it reminds me of being fifteen years old and recovering from heartache, a feeling of nostalgia not unlike hearing a song on the radio and being transported back to a very specific time in my life. Another article of clothing I vividly remember is a T-shirt given to me by my first crush in the sixth grade. It was a tight red V-neck short-sleeved '70s-style shirt with a decal sticker on the front and a picture of a fox that read FOXY LADY. On the back side, in big red felt bubble letters, was my name: JENNY. It was, by far, my favorite shirt of all time, with its powerful message, even though I wasn't sure what "foxy" truly meant. So, I asked my brothers, who were fourteen and seventeen years old at the time, and they told me it meant I was "sexy." I was twelve and knew nothing of what sexy *really* meant.

"What does it mean to be sexy?" I asked. They said it means that boys like the way I moved my body—a pretty provocative thing for a sixth grader to comprehend. But I would wear that T-shirt and strut around my room, swiveling my hips from side to side, owning my walk, and feeling confident about my "foxiness."

So, thank you, Darin Nathan, for bringing out my "sexy," even if the sixth grade is a bit premature and a little inappropriate for a young girl. Today, knowing the power behind what we wear, I'm convinced that that shirt actually began to shape my belief about my own sex appeal.

I wasn't always comfortable in my own skin, though, and spent a good portion of my adolescence in emotional numbness, stumbling around in the dark. Once I got into junior high school, everything changed, and I became super self-conscious and embarrassed of my home life and circumstances. I used my fists as a coping mechanism, which earned me the nickname "Rocky" and got me suspended in junior high and kicked out of high school multiple times.

It's hard to make friends when you are always the new girl in school and all the friend groups have already formed. I learned to adapt to different

types of groups; blending into whatever group would accept me came naturally to me. And while I was able to adapt easily and get along with everyone,
I found that the problem with blending in is that you don't develop your
own sense of identity or personal style. I did not know who I was on the
inside or on the outside, other than broken.

But clothes became a great way for me to try on different "identities."
Like an actor's costume that helps transform her into a character, I used
clothes to help define my own characters. I changed my style frequently
depending on which phase I was in, or what group I was hanging out with—
and I've had many. There was the tough masculine menswear/Doc Martens
tomboy era; the "fashion victim," uber-trendy phase in my teens, wearing
Marciano Guess jeans and anything from the store Contempo Casual;
heavy-metal, hasher style with skin-tight, torn acid-washed jeans, band
T-shirts, leather jackets with patches, and a pack of Marlboro Reds tucked
into the pocket; very girly mixed with preppy; in college, it was all about
being edgy and street-stylish. I could be sporty one day, classic from time to
time, bohemian for a minute. Sexy, both overstated and understated, or edgy
and chic. While I have never been goth or punk, I knew I could blend in
with either group if I needed to, with just a simple change of style.

Like most teenagers, my ability to communicate via my clothes wasn't
particularly unique, even if my circumstances were. My style evolution from
those years has molded mine today: I gravitate toward feminine with a touch
of edgy. Think a floral fit-and-flare dress with a leather jacket, a chunky
Dylanlex necklace, and a Saint Laurent closed-toe pump or ankle booties.
I also lean toward understated sexy staples, like a silk camisole with lace trim,
jeans, a fitted blazer, and a single-strap Manolo Blahnik classic pump. I also
love to incorporate trends with classics for a chic look. Today, I'm consciously
aware that clothes can have a definite impact on the way I feel.

Have you ever noticed that you carry yourself differently when you feel
really good about what you're wearing? When I'm wearing a feminine dress,
I actually don't think I walk, but rather, I *saunter* more gracefully. There's
something about this particular style that activates my divine feminine
energy.

My Bubbie was a classic example of this. As I mentioned before, I spent a lot of time with her, and one of our favorite things to do together was to go to Neiman Marcus and try on hats. Bubbie was very ladylike and would take her time getting herself ready before I would pick her up for our outing together. She would put on one of her best outfits, which usually consisted of a classic Saint John two-piece skirt suit, clip-on earrings (she never did pierce her ears), a pair of nylons (because she never left the house without them), a stunning hat, a Grace Kelly–inspired handle handbag, and a classic, closed-toe, square-heeled Chanel-inspired shoe. She understood the value of investing in good-quality, timeless pieces and used to say, "We are too poor to buy cheap things."

The minute the doorman opened the door for us at Neiman's, she lifted her chin, rotated her shoulders, straightened her back, and sauntered into the department store like she owned the place. I swear, her ninety-year-old body grew an inch and a half taller from her confidence. She exuded more grace and beauty than anyone in that store. When she breezed by, she grabbed the attention of every person. She was like a magnet with her self-assured style and, even at her age, still understood the power behind clothing, never believing she was too old to care about her appearance. She knew exactly what worked for her and owned it.

But you certainly don't have to wait until you're ninety to find it and feel confident in your clothes. The first thing I do with my clients is spend a few hours in their closet, getting to know them and applying my advice from Chapter 3 (taking inventory of the basics and must-haves). I feel honored that they feel comfortable allowing me to be a part of their personal space. A peek into your closet can reveal so much about you. So, I'm always appreciative when someone lets me into their wardrobe. It says they trust me, and I honor that. My job is to identify the missing pieces and help my clients find and stay true to their individual style.

Now, you might be thinking that personal style isn't something you have; let me stop you right there. *Everyone* has it; it's a flawed belief that you don't. *Everyone* I have worked with has a particular style or vibe that resonates with them. But they often just don't know how to apply it to their life and haven't given it much examination or time. My job is to help you find what ignites you and create a wardrobe that is fashionable within that. And I'm also here to let you know that it's okay to have a few different fashion styles that resonate with you. We are humans and multifaceted, and so, too, are our wardrobes. I certainly don't have just *one* style.

But I do believe giving yourself some definitions of the most frequently used fashion styles and visual tools will make it easier for you to identify what you are attracted to and empower you with the right language to communicate that to a salesperson. Once you have identified these styles, it's time to do some "style stalking," as briefly discussed in Chapter 3. Nothing illegal or creepy—simply using social media as a source of style inspiration and a reference guide when shopping. After all, imitation is the highest form of flattery. Personally (and professionally), I use Instagram, Pinterest, department store lookbooks, and magazines.

There are a few things to remember when style stalking. The first is not to "future fantasy shop." I'm notorious for shopping with a friend and saying, "Isn't this great for travel?" I used to have entire sections in my wardrobe for when I would be strolling the streets of Paris in my black-and-white striped sweater, beige trench coat, ballet flats, scarf tied around my neck, and, of course, a beret. I pictured myself sitting in a café, enjoying a glass of sauvignon blanc and a cigarette, or on the bow of a yacht in a gorgeous silk caftan, oversize sun hat, Jackie O sunglasses, sailing through Croatia. The outfits would be picture perfect for the settings dreamed up in my head, except for a few crucial things: I don't particularly like to wear stripes, wine makes me feel sick, I don't smoke (anymore), and I had no upcoming travel plans on my calendar. I'm all about visualizing and fantasizing, but I've decided to keep it real and save time and money and wait until a trip is booked before I shop for it; I would suggest you do the same.

My second suggestion is, when you find looks that you admire for style inspiration, take the time to dissect the photo. Is the model wearing midriff-baring tops with high-waisted slacks? Do you wear either of those? Is the model wearing heels in every picture? Is that realistic for your lifestyle? Would the outfit look the same with a flat, or does it need the heel to complete the look? Is the model wearing an outfit that requires you to wear your hair up so you can see the details of the top of the blouse or dress, and do you wear your hair up? Is the model wearing a skirt above the knee? Is it a low-cut top, and do you feel comfortable wearing that? Basically, does the outfit *fit* your lifestyle? Once you have narrowed down the styles that are realistic for you, create a folder in your phone with the looks you have chosen and bring your Style-list with you when you go shopping. Find an experienced salesperson to help you with your new looks.

Now that you have the *language* to describe what fashion trends excite you, you can show your pictures and communicate your desires easily. It's important to remember that you will probably have a combination of a few styles, and that's perfectly okay. There's no harm in dressing classic one day and bohemian chic the next. Don't be discouraged if you don't find everything in one place; just make sure you purchase from somewhere that has a good return policy. Shopping with your Style-list will ultimately save you time, money, and frustration.

It may take some trial and error to find out who you are, in the fashion sense, and hopefully, by now, you're inspired and ready for a change. Remember: "Change is the law of life." That quote still rings true to me today.

I had no idea I would lose my father when he was just fifty-three years young, or that my Bubbie would live to be one hundred. I couldn't prevent it or predict it. Nothing stays constant. My point is: life is short, so have fun with your fashion. Don't take it too seriously. Your style may evolve over time; actually, I would expect it to. I've changed a lot during my own fashion journey—who knew that those T-shirts would be lodged in my memory, that they would become part of my personal journey, and now, a part of my story? And it's because of my story, I've realized I'm not a chameleon at all— I'm a *unicorn*.

Now, I'll end this chapter with some verbal language and descriptions of different style categories. This will make it easier to describe your vibe to a salesperson the next time you go shopping. And don't forget to Style Stalk me on Instagram: @jenprincipestyles.

The Thirteen Style Categories

1
Classic/Conservative

2
Preppy/East Coast

3
Business Casual

4
Edgy/Rocker

5
Bohemian

6
Sexy

7
Feminine/Girly

8
Men's Inspired/Annie Hall

9
Modest

10
Trendy Chic

11
Modern Minimalist

12
Athleisure Wear/Sportswear

13
Vacation Wear

Classic/Conservative

You can never go wrong with classics. They should be a part of your staple wardrobe because they never go out of style and add an element of timelessness and elegance to your look. A classic bag, trench coat, or loafer can take you a long way. Classic styles are clean and traditional, both timeless and flattering. The cuts of the clothing are simple, and you'll mostly find neutral colors with the occasional pop of color (which could be in the form of a bold-hue lipstick or bright bag). Classics tend not to stand out too much in a crowd but will always look stylish, chic, and put together: think Grace Kelly, Katharine Hepburn, Kate Middleton, Natalie Portman, and Tom Ford.

Classic/Conservative Staples

- Trench or long coat (camel, cream, or black)
- Peacoat
- Classic button-downs in cotton and silk
- Black fitted blazer and oversize blazer
- Navy blazer
- Turtleneck sweaters (black and camel)
- Wide-leg trousers (black and camel)
- Jeans with no holes and no large pockets (fit-and-flare)
- Slacks (white or black); no pockets; clean, flat front
- Cardigans (black, navy, camel, cream)
- Structured bag (black or tan)
- Neck scarf
- Diamond studs
- Closed-toe pumps (black or nude)
- Structured T-shirts (black, gray, or white)
- Denim jacket
- Black leather jacket (keep hardware simple)
- Ballerina slippers
- Loafers

Preppy/East Coast

Preppy style is similar to classic but with more pops of color and bold prints. Taylor Swift and Scott Disick embody this style. Preppy clothes may contain nautical themes and exude a clean-cut image; think of brands like J. Crew, L. L. Bean, and, of course, the iconic Polo Ralph Lauren.

Historically, the term *preppy* was used to describe a subculture of the upper-class youth born into old money—the classic oxford shirt, cable-knit sweater, and loafers. It later evolved into the style of the US Coast elite and became tied to sports like sailing, lacrosse, and rugby. Today, though, we aren't necessarily talking about Ivy Leaguers' fashion, although some of the underlying principles remain. The word *preppy* today is far looser—the "modern preppy" still keeps true to some of the original philosophy, though.

Preppy/East Coast Staples

- Crisp white shirt
- Cardigans
- Striped ¾-sleeve shirt
- Loafers
- Bermuda shorts
- White pants
- Camels and whites
- Polka-dots
  (blouse, skirts, or dresses)
- Checkered or plaid blazer
- Green anorak or army jacket
- Skinny jeans
- Chambray shirtdress
- Denim jacket
- Gingham prints
- Colored pants
- Equestrian-inspired blazer
  or trench coat
  (such as Ralph Lauren)
- Striped dress or tops

Business Casual

Business casual attire can be worn in most offices and can be very stylish and professional. Although the term can vary among workplaces, business casual usually denotes office-appropriate attire. The goal of business casual is for you to feel confident in your workplace and styled in a manner that you would also feel comfortable in meeting friends after work for dinner or drinks without feeling overly businesslike. Aim for a polished look by mixing tailored and traditional pieces with fashion-forward items. Think "Boss Babe" with subtle sex appeal (men's business attire will be covered in Chapter 13).

Business Casual Staples

- Black/gray or pinstripe suit
- Fitted blazers
- Trench coat or waistcoat
- Long sweater or cardigan
- White/navy/camel blouse
- Classic white button-down
- Solid color pencil skirt
- Dark jeans (no holes)
- High-waisted skirts
- Turtleneck blouses
- Camisole
- Flowy dress
- Waist belt
- Wide-leg trousers
- Bold gold and silver chain necklaces
- Closed-toe pump/heeled sandals
- Chic belts and accessories
- Knee-high boots
- Tights

Edgy/Rocker

When we think of edgy fashion, most people think of studded leather jackets, with some mixed metals accessories or a vampy lip. Having an edge to your fashion leaves a lot of room for self-expression: think Gigi Hadid, Madison Beer, and Lady Gaga (although she is on the far end of the spectrum).

And while you may not want to wear a *meat dress* to your next event, adding a little edge to your fashion can be liberating, fun, and powerful. The key here is to own it and love what you wear with confidence. Edgy style means thinking ahead of the curve and wearing pieces that are unique and a little unexpected; for example, Gigi Hadid rocks a luxe, silk hot-pink pajama set with a green metallic shoe and matching clutch for a night out on the town. "Rocker style" can be synonymous with edgy fashion. This is a harder one, as this category changes so fast. But anything goes, as long as it's worn with confidence, which in my opinion, is the true definition of style.

Edgy/Rocker Staples

- Bold statement pieces
- Leather anything
- Leather moto jacket (any color)
- Black skinny jeans (with and without holes)
- Oversize denim jacket
- High-ankle boots
- Metallic boots
- Studded boots
- Rocker T-shirt
- Edgy jewelry
- Smoky makeup
- Plaid shirt
- Bold sunglasses
- Hat (fedora, wide-brimmed Panama, beanies)
- Cool sneakers
- Slip dress or slip skirt
- Tights
- Bold prints and mixed patterns
- Metallics

Bohemian

Bohemian style is generally associated with artists and writers and was initially inspired by the hippies of the '60s and '70s. Dressing bohemian is a way to express yourself and connect with nature. Boho-chic is a style of dressing that is focused on free-flowing fabrics, peasant blouses, fringes, jeweled flats, and sandals. Jewelry that speaks to a *boho look* represents nature and incorporates items like feathers, shells, stones, and wood that can be mixed and layered. For a bohemian vibe, the trick is to mix in the trend with other influences for something subtle. Rachel Zoe is a genius at pulling off a very modern, boho-chic vibe. Mary-Kate and Ashley Olsen, Paris Jackson, and Sienna Miller are also examples of modern boho fashionistas.

Bohemian Staples

- Long, flowy dress or skirt
- Faux fur vests
- Earthy jewelry
- Flared jeans
- Beaded dresses or tops
- Floppy hat
- Embroidered coat
- Ethereal gown
- Western-style belt
- Fringe

Sexy

There's a balance between looking sexy and distasteful. The word *sexy* is so incredibly subjective, so this is clearly just my opinion as a fashionista and personal stylist. There is a time for a plunging neckline and a time to put your boobs away. My rule of thumb is to pick one body part to showcase at a time. If you're wearing a very short skirt to show off your sexy legs, then pair it with a higher-neck blouse or sweater. If you're wearing a top with a plunging neckline and your chest is on display, try pairing it with a longer skirt or slacks. The point is: don't exhibit it *all* at once.

Leather can be very sexy, but to avoid looking like a dominatrix, try pairing with a feminine blouse and/or fitted blazer. I love to dress sexy, and one of the best compliments I can receive is when someone tells me I dress sexy, but that I still look *tasteful*, which has always been one of the goals when dressing myself and my clientele. Remember, too, that sexy is a state of mind. You can dress very conservative and still have sex appeal. In this category, you'll find Jennifer Lopez, Sofía Vergara, and Chrissy Teigen.

Sexy Staples

- Classic slip dress
- Body-con black dress
- Men's oversize jacket
- Black fitted tailored suit
- Lace bodysuit
- Flared slacks
- White or black tight turtleneck
- White silk button-down with lace bra
- Single-strap or Mary Jane heels
- Oversize blazer belted as a dress
- Halter low-cut jumpsuit
- Sexy necklaces
- Hoop earrings
- Lace top
- Leather pencil skirt
- Suit
- Nylons
- Belts to cinch waist

Feminine/Girly

I love feminine flare and girly-girl fashion, the unabashedly feminine wardrobe pieces. For an immediate girly vibe, try a puffed-sleeve blouse or a top with some decorative embellishments. Full skirts that accentuate the waistline or a fit-and-flare dress are sure to bring out your girly girl. When I wear those feminine wardrobe pieces, they bring out my divine feminine energy, something very important to me, especially having grown up in a male-dominant family. It was what literally separated me from the boys! Going head-to-toe feminine might not be your thing, and that's okay. Start small: try pairing a lace top with a black skinny jean or leather pants, or rocking a full skirt with a T-shirt and leather jacket and heels. The idea is to channel the feminine vibe while staying true to your own unique style. Blake Lively and Keira Knightley are in this category.

And it's certainly possible to have a masculine or androgynous vibe to your style yet still exude femininity.

Feminine Staples

- Lace top
- Full skirt
- Fit-and-flare dress
- Butterfly/puffed-sleeve blouses
- Floral dress
- Pleated long skirt
- T-strap shoe
- Tulle skirt
- Pearls
- Delicate jewelry
- Classic bag with handle

Men's Inspired/Annie Hall

Naturally, I must now talk about men's-inspired clothing for women. Borrowing from the masculine classics and incorporating an androgynous edge into your everyday attire or workplace has never been more accepting and fun. The boundaries of men's and women's fashion are becoming more blurred than ever, and with good reason. Fashion is freedom of expression and is no longer gender-specific. Companies are rising to meet the demands of a changing clientele, offering gender-fluid and gender-neutral garments.

Ken Downing, the fashion director of Neiman Marcus, told *The New York Times*, "What we're seeing now is a seismic shift in fashion, a widening acceptance of a style with no boundaries—one that reflects the way young people dress." So, the next time you go out shopping, don't limit yourself to just the women's or men's department.

I have always loved a good men's or women's suit. They are timeless and chic. There's a reason they call it the "power suit": because you feel *powerful* when you wear it. A well-tailored or an oversize suit screams confidence. Try a bold hue or a pinstriped suit for a stylish alternative to the basic black or navy. You can't go wrong with an oversize men's white button-down shirt and jeans, or an oversize boyfriend blazer over a tight body-con dress. A striped button-down with a fitted vest and bold tie paired with a trouser is a stylish and unexpectedly fearless look. And a great pair of suspenders over a blue button-down can cross over from business chic attire to a fun dinner party. Diane Keaton as the iconic Annie Hall, or a more modern version, Victoria Beckham, are both great examples of celebs who rock the menswear-inspired look.

Men's Inspired/Annie Hall Staples

- Oversize suit
- Plaid blazer/
  double-breasted blazer
- Brogues/loafers/monk straps
- Suspenders
- Vests
- White oversize button-down

- Oversize boyfriend blazer
- Tie
- Trench coat
- Hat
- Pinstriped button-down shirt
- Pocket squares

Modest

The definition of *modest* clothing refers to loose clothing, comfortable dressing, and covering the body, sometimes in accordance with one's particular religious or spiritual affiliation or comfort level. Having grown up in an Orthodox Jewish family and having known many practicing Orthodox Jews, Christians, and Mormons (some of whom I have worked with), I know firsthand that sacrificing style is not at all part of most religious beliefs. In fact, although some religions dictate that much of a woman's body be covered, some of the most stylish women I have worked with and know are religious but still emanate femininity, style, grace, and sex appeal. The key here is to invest in outerwear, accessories, shoes, and handbags. You'll find Kate Middleton and Emma Stone in this category.

Modest Staples

- Nylons
- Outerwear
- Long dress
- Dresses below the knee and long sleeves
- Cardigans
- Necktie blouses
- Pencil skirts
- Full skirts
- Belts
- Accessories
- Hats
- Headscarves

Trendy Chic

Having trendy style means your style is up-to-date without the constraints of traditional fashion and that you like to wear all kinds of trends, often at the same time. In my opinion, being *on trend* is important to feeling fashion-forward, but knowing how to add in trends to your wardrobe and what to invest your money in is far more important than being head-to-toe trendy. You could be covered in the latest trends and logos and still lack style. When it comes to the latest seasonal trends, I do my research before investing any money. I like to watch the runway shows for inspiration but sometimes find the clothing unrealistic for my lifestyle. However, I find that the department stores, magazines, and online stores have the latest trends of the season displayed in a realistic and clear-cut way. I make a list of the must-haves for the season and choose a few of those that will enhance my current wardrobe. It then goes on my "shopping list" (different from a Style-list!) and is crossed off my list once I find them.

I am not a slave to fashion, and if I don't think something looks good on me or if I have an aversion to it (overalls and high-rise cropped flare jeans are always a *no* for me), it also means I don't invest money in them. Keep in mind that some things take some time to grow on you too. The high-waisted jean look took a bit of time for me to embrace, especially because I'm short-waisted, but over time I learned how to style them best for my body type and, each season, the jeans were made slightly more flattering.

Once I found the right designer for my body type, all bets were off, and I invested in pieces in all the basic colors. I tend to spend my big dollars on classic pieces like a shoe, bag, or coat and purchase my trendier items at my favorite mainstream stores, like Zara, Revolve, H&M, or Storets.

Naturally, the next question is, How long will something stay in style? It's difficult to predict how long an item will stay in fashion. For example, the boyfriend jean came back in 2010, skinny jeans in 2011, and high-waisted skinny jeans in 2015. The basic ankle bootie has been going strong for a decade, although the toe shape has changed from round to pointy. While the choker necklace was on the cover of every magazine in 2016, it came and went in just a blink of an eye. I would say the general rule of thumb for something very trendy is three to five years. So, will the low-waisted jeans be back? Yes, they most certainly will, following the so-called *twenty-year cycle of fashion*. And, when they reappear, they're usually much improved upon as a result of better materials, more enticing silhouettes, and intricate details.

So, you may be asking what trends you should invest in. My answer is what you can afford and what looks good on you! Spending money on the "It" bag can add a lot of bang for your buck but may or may not stay around for decades to come. So, choose wisely. For inspiration on all things trendy, see Wendy Nguyen, Danielle Bernstein, and Aimee Song.

Trendy Chic Staples (from 2019 to 2022)

- Animal prints
- Cropped blazers
- Cowboy boots
- Top handle bags with scarves tied around handle
- Crochet and macramé bags
- Kitten heels
- Neons and pastels
- Crossbody bags and fanny packs
- Faux fur oversize coats
- Vinyl shoes and bags
- Platform sneakers
- Over-the-top ruffles
- Puffed sleeves
- Colorful leather or pleather

Modern Minimalist

Elegant but unfussy. The concept behind the minimalist is all about choosing simplicity over standing out without sacrificing style. The looks are elegant but unfussy with minimum effort and maximum impact. The modern minimalist's wardrobe is like the Classic/Conservative genre but paired way down. Simple, clean lines and sleek silhouettes; neutrals and tonal dressing are the central concept. Modern minimalists aren't afraid to wear loose, oversize pieces or boxy silhouettes, and they love to layer. Think Carolyn Bessette-Kennedy, Cate Blanchett, Sade, Jennifer Aniston, and Gwyneth Paltrow.

Modern Minimalist Staples

- Car coat or trench coat
- Wide-leg trousers
- Knit dress
- Midi skirt (knee-length skirt)
- A chunky, oversize knit sweater

- Shirt dress (boxy)
- Oversize cotton button-down
- Knit tanks
- Loafers

Athleisure Wear/Sportswear

Being from Southern California, athletic wear is a huge trend and staple in my wardrobe. Whether you're planning to hit the gym or not, athleisure wear has taken over the fashion market because it's flattering, easy to wear, and comfortable. I would also like to add here that clothing carries symbolic meaning, and when you put on a pair of workout pants, it primes the brain to behave in ways that are consistent with the meaning behind them (e.g., putting on your workout clothes is a great way to get your brain thinking about exercise).

It's not unusual for me to leave my house, hit the weights in the morning, and head straight from the gym to shop or work with a client. Therefore, I invest a little time and money in my runaround clothes so I don't feel frumpy during the day. My activewear clothes have also become a staple for me when I travel. I can use my shiny leggings with a silk blouse, a blazer, and heels for a night out or wear them with a big chunky sweater and boots during the day. My typical airport outfit is a pair of fashionable and comfortable workout pants, a graphic tank top, jean or leather jacket, and some fun sneakers. So, if you're all about comfort and consider yourself casual but don't want to sacrifice looking put together while running around town, then consider investing in some stylish athletic wear.

Athleisure Wear/Sportswear Staples and Brands

- Lululemon
- Beyond Yoga
- Koral
- Alo
- Enza Costa
- Tracksuit
- Joggers
- Shapewear leggings (from brands like Spanx or Skims)
- Leggings (multiple colors)
- Tank tops
- Long-sleeve pullover
- Fitted hoodie
- Zip-up jacket
- Puffer vest
- Jean jacket
- Seamless long-sleeve T-shirt (for layering)
- Windbreaker
- Bomber jacket
- Long sweater 3/4-length (for fuller figures)
- Duster sweater (for fuller figures)
- Cool sneakers

Vacation Wear

Who doesn't love to go on vacation but dread the packing? I am not going to pretend that I don't overpack. I do! I still can't seem to find a way to bring fewer than five pairs of shoes with me whenever I travel. I have, however, mastered the art of reusing my clothes to recreate an entirely new look. Packing can be an overwhelming task, so here are a few things that can help set your expectations and make it easier to look your best when on vacay.

First, block out an hour of uninterrupted time to pack. Next, depending on where you're traveling to, start by using the list below and pulling out all the items you know for certain will be going on the trip with you (e.g., if you're planning a trip to Hawaii, your bathing suit, cover-ups, hat, and sunglasses are no-brainers). Then, write down your daily agenda and lay out the outfits you plan on wearing that day and include shoes, your jewelry, and bag.

Try to pick neutrals for your bag and shoes so they can be reused. Take a photograph of each outfit. This will help you to stay organized and not pack too much. I like to use large reusable bags and smaller ones to hold my accessories (which I can later use for dirty clothes and wet bathing suits). Try to rewear your jeans, leggings, or your basic dresses. One easy way to create a completely new look is by using different accessories and outerwear and changing your hairstyle. A long, black flowy dress with a bright pashmina scarf, gold earrings, and sandals can look completely different with turquoise jewelry and a jean jacket. Here are some of the essential items I have found that work well when traveling.

Vacation Wear Staples

Warm weather:
- Carry-on fashionable beach bag or tote
- Bathing suit (one-piece and two-piece)
- Beach cover-up
- Accessories, including fun jewelry like colorful earrings or statement necklaces
- Travel hat (put in carry-on)
- Workout pants (shiny or dressy)
- Scarf (to tie around neck or hat)
- Scarf or pashmina to wear over shoulders at night
- Stylish sunglasses
- Lightweight sweater or jean jacket
- Flat thong-style sandals
- Wedges
- Fashionable sneakers
- Crossbody bag or fanny pack
- Basic sundresses

Cold weather:
- Carry-on fashionable tote bag
- Trench coat or long coat
- Turtleneck (fitted black, cream, camel, or red)
- Black, camel, or cream coat
- Pashmina
- Heavier scarf
- Walking boots (block heel)
- Sunglasses
- Long-sleeve fitted shirts for layering
- Puffer vest or jacket
- High-heel boots
- Closed-toe pumps
- Loafers or brogues
- Tights
- Chunky sweater
- Workout pants
- Duster sweater
- Warm hat
- Felt hat for fashion
- Leather gloves
- Fitted long-sleeve dress
- Jeans (black and blue)
- Flare faux fur jacket or vest
- Diamond stud earrings

Did you resonate with a particular fashion trend but never knew how to describe your vibe to a salesperson? Having the right terminology will be very helpful the next time you go shopping and you're looking for the modern minimalistic shirt dress or the boho-chic maxi dress. Language is the key to fully expressing yourself, both in the fashion world and in life.

CHAPTER 8

Let's Play Baseball

"The most potent muse of all is our own inner child."

—Stephen Nachmanovitch

When my son Jeremy was five years old, he would lay his clothes out on the floor in the shape of a little boy every night before going to bed. Monday he would lay out his baseball pants, a long-sleeve thermal with his jersey over it, cleats stuffed with baseball socks, a glove on his right, a bat on his left, and, of course, his baseball hat. He was a *baseball boy*. Tuesday, neatly arranged on his floor, would lay his soccer shorts, shin guards, soccer cleats, ADIDAS socks, a sweat headband, and soccer ball. He was a *soccer boy*. Wednesday was a football jersey, shoulder pads, football pants, and a football. He was a *football boy*.

Each night, Jeremy picked a different theme that dictated what he would wear the following day. One night, I came into his room to tuck him into bed and carefully stepped over the young bodiless "boy" who lay on his floor and looked down to see something I hadn't seen before. There lay a suit, a tie (which was far too big for him), a nice dress shirt, dress shoes, socks inside the shoes, and a briefcase lying next to his suit.

I looked over at him and asked, "Jeremy, what are you going to be tomorrow?"

"I'm going to be an important businessman, just like Dad," he replied.

What Jeremy was subconsciously doing was brilliant. Jeremy wanted to *feel* like a baseball boy, he wanted to *feel* like a football player, he wanted to *feel* like a soccer boy, and he wanted to *feel* like a powerful businessman, so he dressed himself accordingly to identify with and *become* what he had imagined.

When we put on an item of clothing, it's common that the wearer adopts the characteristics associated with said piece of clothing. There have been numerous psychological studies that support the idea that *what we wear* can transform *how we feel*. The term *enclothed cognition* is the phenomenon that describes the effect clothing has on the cognitive process. What we wear can affect our psychological states and change how we feel, behave, and perform tasks. So, the effects of clothes extend way beyond covering and protecting our bodies.

Hajo Adam and Adam D. Galinsky from Northwestern University conducted several fascinating studies that support this theory.[4] One study entailed giving a group of people doctors' coats, while others wore ordinary street clothes. They were then asked to perform a series of tasks, followed by another test for selective attention that measured their abilities to notice incongruities. The participants wearing the lab coats made half as many errors as those wearing their street clothes. In a second test, two sets of people were given lab coats. One group was told their lab coats were doctors' coats and the other, that they were painters' coats. They were then given a series of visual tasks to spot minor differences in pictures and, once again, the ones in doctors' coats found far more differences than those wearing the painters' coats, indicating heightened sustained attention.

Children, like Jeremy at that age, are a wonderful example of this phenomenon. Have you ever watched a young child play dress-up and engage in dramatic role-playing, transforming into a princess, a dragon, or a superhero? They are subconsciously ascribing meaning to the article of clothing that they are wearing based on their own past experiences. And while children do this subconsciously, there are many industries that understand the psychological impact of wardrobe. Theater and television are the leaders in understanding image and assuming the identity and persona of a character through wardrobe.

Think about some of the very first costumes in ancient plays, like masks depicting whether the play was a comedy or a tragedy. On Broadway, actors don their costumes during rehearsals months before a show debut. This immersion allows the actor to get into a mindset where they can fully

---

4 Hajo Adam and Adam D. Galinsky, "Enclothed Cognition," ScienceDirect, July 2012, https://www.sciencedirect.com/science/article/abs/pii/S0022103112000200.

encompass the character they are portraying. The costumes also create a story and communicate, without words, social status, religious beliefs, and personality traits of the characters. They can tell us who a character is and their behaviors without the use of verbal communication.

The same is true in movies, where clothing can be as much of a character as the actors on-screen. Julia Roberts in *Pretty Woman* undergoes an entire demeanor change after going on a shopping spree in Beverly Hills, where she suddenly becomes the owner of a new, sophisticated, stylish, and expensive wardrobe (which I am not suggesting you need, by the way!). She becomes instantly more refined and ladylike thanks to her wardrobe change. And then there's the scene with her wearing the iconic polka-dot dress with a hat and gloves at the polo match. At first fidgety and insecure, she pulls her chin up, fixes her dress, and walks with total confidence onto the polo field. *Sex and the City* is another wonderful example, clearly depicting four completely different characters through wardrobe: sexy Samantha, serious lawyer Miranda, feminine preppy Charlotte, and, of course, New York fashionista Carrie.

I have always been fascinated by TV and movie wardrobes; I would watch movies and dramas simply to fixate on the *clothes*. The endless details of fabric choices, different era styles, period pieces, jewelry, hair, makeup choices, even the scene setting that complemented the wardrobe choices, and the way the clothes defined each character.

The importance of clothing even extends into the world of sports, where uniforms are significant for a number of reasons. Why is a uniform vital to the success of a team, and what happens to us, the viewer, when we wear our favorite baseball jersey or hat to a game? Humans are inherently tribal and want to feel like we belong. A sports uniform sends a message to the brain of unity, cohesiveness, and being part of a team, of brotherhood/sisterhood and loyalty—*uniforms* represent something bigger than just identification. When we wear a member of our favorite team's jersey, we are connecting and supporting the team, becoming part of that tribal sense of belonging and *feeling* like we're part of them.

Uniforms can also command respect. Police, firefighters, military members, and others have a certain discernible change in their mindset when dressed in uniform. Most uniformed services sanctify their uniforms, with individuals earning the right to wear parts of them through hard work and sacrifice. The perfectly pressed shirts, belts, polished boots, hats, glistening badges, and medals are all what they represent: integrity, loyalty, duty, respect, and courage. It also communicates that a person is able to manage life's troubles and can be counted on, which may explain why, to some people, a person in uniform is viewed as *very desirable.*

My mother-in-law sure thought so. My stepfather-in-law served in the navy during World War II, and I will never forget when he passed away, when his military brothers came to "flag" him. Two men in full uniform came to my mother-in-law's home at 4:30 in the morning. They saluted her, entering the home at a synchronized pace. They covered his body with a sheet and placed the American flag over it, stood in salute, and said, "On behalf of the President of the United States, and a grateful nation, please accept this flag as a symbol of our appreciation for your loved one's honorable and faithful service."

They then folded the flag in ceremonial fashion and handed it to her, turned on their heels, and left her home. It still brings tears to my eyes when I think about it. I will always remember the overwhelming feeling I had of respect and gratitude as I watched those two men stand fully adorned in the same uniform that my stepfather-in-law once wore with pride as he fought for our country. It literally took my breath away.

Another set of uniforms that commands respect is that of the clergy. A priest wears a white "Roman collar," or white band that encircles the neck, and is one of the most distinctive and universally identifiable pieces of clothing among Catholics. Orthodox rabbis wear black suits and *kippot* (head covering) or a *shtreimel* (a type of fur hat); clothing has always played a significant role in Judaism.

And while all these symbolic articles of clothing create a sense of identity, connection, and affiliation with their professional, religious, or personal lives, sadly, stripping one's identity has also played a significant role in history. During World War II, the Nazis stripped every prisoner, shaved their entire bodies, including the hair on their heads, and took every personal belonging from victims—even eyeglasses and wedding rings—so that nobody had any sense of their own personal identity. My grandmother lost her family in the war, and I still remember how upset she would become when I would cut my hair. I'm not sure if there was any connection, but I suspect there might have been.

Now you understand the *meaning* and *messages* that lie behind the clothes we wear, and how they can impact our lives. On a professional level, clothes play a vital role, but they equally impact us on a personal and even sexual level.

I get more calls for my services from newly single men and women than from any other type of client. Why is it that when we are single or starting to date someone, we suddenly decide to invest more time, effort, and money into our wardrobes? It's because, subconsciously, we know that when we feel good in what we wear, the more confident and self-assured we become. What we wear has a direct correlation to how we feel. Another reason that we dress up for dating is because we want to make a good, lasting impression. So, then, it's fair to say that dressing up and investing in your wardrobe can not only change how you feel and behave, but it can also have an impact on others.

I remember when I first started dating my husband Tony. My wardrobe budget significantly went up, and the red dress I splurged on was well worth the lasting impression it made on him, now after twenty-five years of marriage. Interestingly, I chose to wear red without consciously knowing the psychology behind colors. Turns out, according to research, men are more attracted to women who wear red, and it seems women who want to attract men do so by wearing the bold hue. Apparently, Chris de Burgh knew the effects of a woman in red because he wrote the hit song, "Lady in Red," which topped the charts in twenty-five countries. One of my favorite things to do is convert a client from wearing only black and white to adding a little color into their wardrobe.

I'm not claiming to be a therapist by any means, although there's something about being in a client's closet and working with someone in their personal wardrobe that creates an intimacy that allows my clients to open up to me about their private lives. I've had women cry to me that they don't feel attractive anymore or don't feel good about themselves, and men claim that they feel they've lost their mojo. But after working with me and investing

more effort into their outer appearances, they express how much more confident they feel in their private lives and, as a result, are dating more frequently.

Married clients stand to benefit from revamped wardrobes too. I'm so
happy when a potential client, who's married, reaches out because it means
they're open to putting in additional effort into their appearance. I have had
both husbands and wives thank me when their spouses start getting their
mojos back and are looking and feeling more confident.

Of course, this doesn't mean that a marriage could also benefit from some
solid therapy and work. But clothes can play a significant role in boosting
those "trouble areas," whether it's helping with sexual confidence or overall
self-esteem. But for those opposed, there certainly is a philosophical hostility
toward the fashion world. My middle brother is a great example of this. He
eventually stopped using the color-coded hangers that I had "Garanimaled"
for him and, in high school, developed intense contempt and anger toward
the fashionable "superficial" crowd. His claim was that they were shallow
and only cared about appearances.

I have heard a myriad of reasons as to why fashion is "shallow," and that
people shouldn't be judged by what they wear; that it's what's *on the inside*
that matters most. Some may think that fashion is just profligate indulgence
and that our vibrant personalities will detract the attention away from our
dull attire.

But think again.

I also hear that fashion is frustrating, time-consuming, and expensive.
But it's my goal with this book to address these misconceptions; to manage
your time (by creating your shopping list), alleviate frustration (by finding a
professional, either in a department store or hiring a stylist), and creating a
realistic budget for purchasing long-term investment pieces while adding in
some inexpensive, trendier pieces.

Sure, the material world can be considered shallow. But that's a very
broad statement to make, and it doesn't take into consideration the value
that looking your best can bring to those who need it and understand its
purpose. Of course, it's what's on the inside that matters most, but denying
the significance and impact that clothes can have on a person doesn't honor

that appearance can have a place in personal transformation too. Clothes, shoes, bags, jewelry, makeup, and even hair shouldn't define you, but they can help shape parts of your identity and strengthen or open up parts of you that you didn't even know existed. Balance is the goal.

My middle brother graduated high school, became a doctor, and earned the right to wear a doctor's lab coat—his favorite piece of clothing. However, since high school, he has come around to the power of fashion. And although he's frugal and hates to spend the money, he has found a balance that works for him and his girlfriend, who appreciates the extra effort he puts into looking put together. She tells him that it's a turn-on when he ditches his graphic tees for a nice button-down. Like I've always said: a well-dressed man is fashion foreplay for women.

As for Jeremy and his baseball uniform, he continued his love of baseball and wore a uniform throughout his junior high and high school years. What he unconsciously knew as a little boy about clothes creating a feeling to get you into a mindset, today he is even more deliberate in his wardrobe choices, as he's now in the dating world and beginning his career path. We still have his first baseball jersey framed with a picture of him wearing it hanging in his room. And when I go into his empty room today and see it hanging there, I'm reminded of the little "boy" lying across the floor next to his bed, just waiting for a person to bring him to life. Perhaps we all need to tap into our inner child a little more and allow clothes to create the *feeling* that can help create the reality.

VIDEO TUTORIALS

CHAPTER 9

Judge a Book by Its Cover

*"Opportunity is missed by most people
because it was dressed in overalls and looks like work."*

—Thomas Edison

Clothing can play a vital role to your overall success and how others in business perceive you. Whether you already have a job or are wanting to grow your business, every detail about your personal presentation communicates something specific and may influence whether someone wants to hire you or do business together more than you think. What we communicate through our clothing, intentionally or not, is powerful. Clothing is one of the primary instruments in creating a positive first impression, and since our clothing tells a clear story about us, making that first impression is invaluable. Remember: "You never get a second chance to make a first impression."

We've all heard, "Don't judge a book by its cover," and it speaks to not making snap judgments before we have a better, more holistic understanding of what we are presented with. And while I would like to think that we don't do this, and that we get to know someone's character before making such judgments, I also know that that's just not realistic. This can be especially true in business where we may not have the luxury of time.

The truth is, the cover is literally designed to sell you on its contents. It contains the title and author and, on the back, endorsements and a summary or something about the author. The cover's entire purpose is to grab your attention and interest you enough to get you to purchase it. You are the "cover" of your own book. Think of it as the branding you'll use to "sell" yourself for your next job or big business deal.

Psychology studies reveal that first impressions are formed within the first seven to seventeen seconds of meeting someone, and 55 percent of an opinion is determined by physical appearance.[5] So, since you only have a short window to impress a potential employer or future business partner, it's best to make sure that your personal "cover" is recognizable, memorable, and at its *best*. The goal is to create a cover that makes you feel confident and gets people to notice you and "buy" your book.

Forbes published an article in June 2018 called, "You and Your Business Have 7 Seconds to Make a First Impression" and how that time span is getting even shorter.[6] This speaks to the importance of outer appearances having a larger role than you may think to landing that dream job or closing that deal. Studies have shown that when you dress up, you're also sending a message to those around you that you care about details and take pride in your work. It also says, "I'm a prepared and ready person." In another study by Yale in 2014, 128 participants between the ages of eighteen and thirty-two were given mock negotiations of buying and selling.[7] Those dressed poorly averaged a theoretical profit of $680,000, while those dressed professionally and in business suits earned an average profit of $2.1 million, while the neutral-dressed group averaged a profit of $1.5 million. According to the coauthor of the study, the poorly dressed participants deferred to the suited ones, and the suited participants could sense this heightened respect and backed down less than they might have otherwise.

"Dress for success" is more than just an empty feel-good aphorism; it's science. There is scientific proof that what you wear has a direct correlation with your creativity, job performance, confidence, and overall success. Remember the study with the lab coats and the street clothes in Chapter 6?

---

5 Jackie Rakers, "What Makes a Good First Impression," *IOM Blog*, March 10, 2016, https://institute.uschamber.com/what-makes-a-good-first-impression.
6 Serenity Gibbons, "You And Your Business Have 7 Seconds To Make A First Impression: Here's How To Succeed," Forbes, June 19, 2018, https://www.forbes.com/sites /serenitygibbons/2018/06/19/you-have-7-seconds-to-make-a-first-impressi on-heres-how-to-succeed.
7 Dennis Green, "It turns out that dressing well can actually make you more successful," February 26, 2016, https://www.businessinsider.com/dressing-for-success-actually -works-2016-2.

A study from Northwestern University researchers examined a concept called "enclothed cognition," which is defined in their report as "the systematic influence that clothes have on the wearer's psychological processes" or "the mental changes that we undergo when we wear certain clothes."[8] In other words, as much as your clothes say something about you, they are also saying something *to* you.

"Enclothed cognition" refers to the idea that you should dress not just how you feel, but how you *want* to feel. Ever wonder why it's called a "power suit"? It's because it makes you feel powerful when you wear it.

Another common adage is, "Dress for the job you *want*, not the job you *have*." In fact, some Fortune 500 companies have a policy that employees are to follow the dress code of senior leadership. According to a *Forbes* article, how you dress at work sends a number of signals about how you view the environment, how much respect you have for your work and yourself, what groups you identify with, and where you think you belong.[9] But this doesn't mean conforming to the standard office culture.

In my experience with both Millennial and Gen Zers (I happen to have one of each), most of them don't want to conform to the standard office wear, as dictated by what we see on Wall Street. Instead, they want to wear suits only when they want to, not because they have to. This is especially true in the tech world, where casual (think hoodies and denim) is the norm and business attire, a rarity.

Which is all to say that, even if standards and norms have changed, being cognizant of how you present yourself to the world and the opportunities that could come from that presentation hasn't. If you want extraordinary results, then be prepared by dressing the part. Even in 2009 after the recession, Facebook's Mark Zuckerberg committed himself to wearing a tie every day for a full year before retiring them in exchange for his iconic gray plain

---

8 Emily VanSonnenberg, "Enclothed Cognition: Put On Your Power!" Positive Psychology News, May 21, 2012, https://positivepsychologynews.com/news/emily -vansonnenberg/2012052122126.

9 Bernie Klinder, "Should People Really Dress For The Job They Want, Not The Job They Have?" Forbes, November 18, 2018, https://www.forbes.com/sites/quora/2018/11/15 /should-people-really-dress-for-the-job-they-want-not-the-job-they-have/?sh=448391582636.

T-shirt attire. He said, "After the start of a recession in 2008, I wanted to signal to everyone at Facebook that this was a serious year for us."

I read an article in *Forbes* with a piece of advice given by a CEO of a Fortune 500 company that stated, "If you want to climb the corporate ladder, then dress as if every day you were on an interview."[10] Great advice, but how do we bridge the gap today between an older, more conservative generation accustomed to business attire with the younger, current generations whose standards are much more casual and individualistic?

I think the solution lies in understanding what standards your particular industry has set and utilizing your own individuality within those standards to create your personalized "book cover." And, for younger generations, remembering that "casual" doesn't mean "sloppy." It's perfectly okay to add your own flare and push the boundaries while keeping things professional, but also *know your audience*. What might be perfectly acceptable in the office might not convey the right message to a more conservative client.

Let's go back to *Pretty Woman*. As you know, Julia Roberts plays Vivian, a sex worker. One of my favorite scenes is when Edward, played by Richard Gere, gives her cash to go shopping in Beverly Hills for some "proper clothes," knowing that they will be attending some upcoming business dinners. Vivian is treated poorly because of her appearance, and the saleswoman refuses to help her, assuming she can't afford their clothes. The saleswoman eventually asks Vivian to leave.

When she returns to the hotel empty-handed and tells Edward what happened, he escorts her back to Beverly Hills. The owners of the store recognize him in his well-tailored suit, of course, and instantly, Vivian is treated like royalty. On her way back to the hotel, she visits the store that had asked her to leave, walks up to the saleswoman, and asks her if she remembers her from the other day. When the saleswoman finally places her, Julia holds up her bags and says, "Big mistake. Big. Huge." I love a good revenge story, but what I love most is the instantaneous change in her overall confidence and demeanor once she adorned herself with more ladylike, conservative clothing.

10 Bernie Klinder, "Should People Really Dress for the Job They Want, Not the Job They Have?" *Forbes*, November 15, 2018, https://www.forbes.com/sites/quora/2018/11/15/should-people-really-dress-for-the-job-they-want-not-the-job-they-have/?sh=448391582636.

This chapter is dedicated to my sons, one of whom is a Millennial and the other, a Gen Z. They are getting ready to go out into the world and begin their careers, set to discover their own unique paths and God-given purpose. I recognize that, in some ways, the work that goes into building their personal brands is harder than when my generation was coming up. Social media platforms are literally at their fingertips. While it's important to brand yourself and care about the cover of your book, it's also hard to resist comparing yourself to others and their depictions of their seemingly perfect lives. As Theodore Roosevelt so eloquently put it, "Comparison is the thief of joy."

Pictures depicting wealth, private jets, travel, perfect bodies, parties (some of which you're not invited to), ex-significant others in new relationships, yachts, and exotic cars can generate excessive envy—jealousy, even. And when it comes to fashion and *influencing*, the number of likes and followers an account has, or flashy pictures of a blogger showing off the new "It" bag can make us feel like we're constantly not measuring up; even when that so-called reality exists only on the internet.

I like to remind myself that even salt can look like sugar. So, while I've advised judging a book by its cover when it's our *own* cover (and we're trying to further our professional lives), remember sometimes a cover is just a cover. And it might look like that cover has its shit together, but in reality, that couldn't be further from the truth.

I must confess, I, too, have been guilty of judging a book by its cover. One summer, I was asked to attend a three-day women's wellness retreat in Northern California with my soul sister Rebecca. The campus was nestled among majestic, ancient redwood trees and sequoias. I felt humbled just being in their massive presence. I learned that these gigantic trees have tiny cones about one inch long to spread their seeds around but also have large root systems often extending one hundred miles, which then intertwine with the roots of other redwoods in the forest.

I find that piece of information extraordinarily fascinating. To the naked eye, we can't see the roots below the surface, spanning those hundred miles, the trees depending on each other for survival. Equally mind-blowing is that these enormous trees have lived for thousands of years and will continue to live well past my own lifetime and yours. It made me consider my own mortality and how very short our time really is here on this earth. I wondered about the people and the species before me who have stumbled upon these very same trees, who they were and what role they played during their time on earth.

At that moment, I felt a deep connection to the earth. I felt as though I was meant to be there in the forest, acknowledging that our lives may be short, but that we are all connected. As I walked through the forest and brushed my fingers across the trees, I felt nostalgic, as I started to reminisce about my childhood, when I loved to walk and be in nature. I remembered how I could walk for hours as a child, singing and connecting to earth and how, even as a young child, I needed this time to connect to the source and listen to my soul.

I then heard Rebecca say, "Jen, let's head back and clean up before the next lecture," waking me from my reverie. That first night at the welcome meeting, Rebecca and I sat in a room with two hundred other women from all different backgrounds and places. Various lectures were held simultaneously, with people splintering off to whatever piqued their interest and could answer the specific wellness questions they had.

I was there because Rebecca, a holistic practitioner and one of the smartest women I know, had invited me. While I didn't have any specific wellness questions or quandaries in mind, I figured a mind-opening weekend together couldn't hurt the mind, body, and soul. On that very first night upon entering the lecture hall, we were told to write our full names on pieces of paper and place them into the basket at the check-in table. After the welcome lecture, one of the doctors, and leaders of the retreat, held up the basket and asked that we draw a name from the basket. The name of that person would be our "angel" for the weekend.

"You do not need to go searching for your angel, and don't worry if you don't find your angel or your angel doesn't find you. There is no right or wrong, and there's nothing that you need to be doing. We encourage you to just relax and let the universe do the work for you," the leader reassured us.

So, when the basket made its way over to me, I reached in and pulled out a name: Jill Fremont. I was excited about the prospect of finding my angel, or her finding me, and equally excited about being someone else's angel. I wondered what it all meant. By evening's end, we had dispersed, with some headed to the cafe, others to sit around the fireplace, and some back to their rooms. I could hear strangers introducing themselves to one another and wondered if anyone had already made an angelic connection that first night. Tired but inspired, I retreated to my room for the evening.

The next morning, I woke up very early. I looked over at my phone; it was 5:30 A.M. Nevertheless, I was wide awake and wanted a cup of coffee. Rebecca was still sleeping, so I quietly put on my Alexander Wang matching sweatsuit, grabbed my Moncler beanie and scarf, put on my Stan Smith sneakers, slicked on some lip gloss, and slipped out of the room, heading toward the café for a fresh cup of java.

Everything was quiet, except for the chirping of birds. There was no one in sight. The wind whipped through the trees, and the air was bone-chillingly cold. I wrapped my scarf tightly around my neck and could see my breath in the chilled air as I walked toward the fireplace. As I approached the flames, there was one woman sitting with her back toward me. I walked past her and pulled on the doors to the café, but they were locked.

"They don't open for another half an hour," I heard a voice say.

I turned around. "Oh, okay, I guess we're the early birds in the group," I replied.

I saw the source of the voice, the woman who had her back toward me, and took a seat across from her. Awkward silence. "Wow, it's cold this morning," I said.

"Uh-huh," she replied.

"It smells so fresh outside, and the air feels so clean," I continued.

"Uh-huh."

After a closer look, I took a quick inventory of my loquacious conversation partner. She looked like she literally just rolled out of bed. Her hair was a disheveled mess, she was wearing oversize flannel pajama pants, a hooded Disneyland Mickey Mouse sweatshirt two sizes too big, and a pair of worn-out Ugg slippers with a hole in one toe.

"Have you been here before?" I asked.

"Nope, this is my first time," she replied curtly.

"Where are you from?" I asked.

"I'm from Wasco, California."

"Oh, I'm not sure I've ever heard of that." Silence again. She wasn't very inquisitive or talkative, the worst kind of random stranger. After a few minutes of sitting and staring into the fire, I looked at my watch. We still had twenty minutes before caffeine was a possibility.

"What do you do in Wasco?" I asked.

"I work at a postal office," she replied.

"Oh, it must be busy this time of the year."

Again, silence. By this time, it was deafening.

"I live in LA. I'm a wardrobe stylist," I said, unprompted.

She laughed. "Of *course* you are."

I felt judged—who was she to judge my career?

"I could use a stylist. Do you just wake up looking like that?" She laughed.

Well, no, I thought. It took me a couple of extra minutes. Undeterred, I stood up, leaned over, and put my hand out.

"I'm Jen, by the way. I never introduced myself," I said.

"Hi, I'm Jill," she replied.

"Jill? As in Jill Fremont?" I had to ask.

"Yes, I am," she replied.

I told her she was "my angel," to which, of course, she laughed. We attempted conversation for the next few minutes, but it felt forced. I have to be honest: I was disappointed in my angel. I had fantasized that when I pulled her name from the basket the night before, we would have an immediate soul connection and form a lifelong friendship. The only thing that was clear to me was that we had little in common except waking up early and a coffee addiction.

Oh, well, I thought. I was still someone else's angel to be found and maybe it would all make more sense in the following days.

The door to the café unlocked, we stood up, smiled, and headed in for our morning beverages. Jill and I went our separate ways, and the weekend continued as scheduled. We saw each other several times during workshops and smiled but made no additional effort to force a connection. During the weekend, I was approached by several people asking if I was Susan or Diane or Laura but never asked if I was Jen. I was never "found."

On the final day of the retreat, there was a closing ceremony in the large auditorium. The room had floor-to-ceiling windows with a view of the exquisite redwoods. The sun, aglow with brilliant orange and red hues, had just started to set. It was a perfect ending to a magical, informative, and peaceful retreat with my soul sister. I didn't come seeking answers and, so far, the weekend proved to be informative and interesting. The instructors welcomed us into the room as a soft, melodic drumbeat rolled in the background and the scent of patchouli wafted through the air.

Six sets of parallel lines, made from masking tape, roughly four feet from each other, ran down the length of the room. We were instructed to find our angels and stand on the tape. People scurried around the room looking for their angels, Jill and I finding each other immediately. Jill never found her other angel, and my angel never found me, so it was just the two of us as we waited for our next set of instructions. Once the room had settled down and everyone was in their right place, the instructor told us that she would be giving a series of statements. If we felt connected to the statement, then we were to take one small step forward toward our angel and then step back onto the black tape. If we related to the statement strongly, we were to take a larger step forward, wait several seconds, and then take a step back onto the black tape. There were only two primary rules to the exercise: 1) absolutely no judgments and 2) eye contact had to be kept with your angel at all times.

But before any questions could be asked and "answered," the instructor would guide us through a group meditation. The drumroll grew slightly louder as she began. She asked us to close our eyes and breathe through our noses and exhale through our mouths, as her partner chanted a ceremonial mantra.

As the drumming grew louder, I could feel my breath begin to slow and flow in synchronized harmony to the beat. The vibration of the drums pulsated through my body. First came some calming and positive affirmations and then several directives:

"There is no judgment in this room," the instructor said deliberately, pausing to let the words soak in. The drums moved from my right eardrum to my left as the drummer moved around the room.

"We do not feel sorry for anyone." Pause.

"There is no shame here." *Boom. Boom. Boom.*

The drums continued beating louder as they began to sing and hum. "You are loved." Drums beating faster. "You are exactly where you're supposed to be." *Boom, boom.* A gong echoed and vibrated throughout the room. "You are safe." The drums suddenly softened to a slow and steady tempo. She then instructed us to open our eyes and keep our gaze upon our partner for the remainder of the questions.

Then there was a moment of silence before the first statement. And then the dance began. At first, the statements and questions were general and broad but soon became more intimate and intense as we peeled back the layers of emotion.

"I have a job." Jill and I stepped forward and back. The same went for the next statements: "I have a sibling" and "I am in a relationship." When it came to "I have found my soul mate," though, I was the only one who stepped forward.

For a moment, I felt a twinge of sadness for her. But then remembered the rules: no judgments. "I have children." Me, forward and back.

"I want children." She stepped forward, then back. We continued staring into each other's eyes.

"I have lost a parent." I could feel my heart beating faster and harder. I began to feel self-conscious as I stepped forward and then back.

"I was abandoned by a parent." That would be one big step forward for me.

Staring into Jill's eyes, I could feel a palpable connection as we waded through the choreography of this intimate dance. "I have lost a sibling." Jill took a big step forward. I swallowed hard, holding back tears. "I have lost a child." We both stood still, but I could see in my periphery my neighbor step forward. My heart felt like someone was squeezing the life out of it.

"I have lost someone I love to suicide."

We both took a large step forward.

Jill's eyes began to water. It was now terrifying keeping our eyes locked on one another.

"I have thought about suicide."

Jill took a large step forward. She took her eyes off me and looked down at the ground for a moment. I could feel her shame and embarrassment.

Tears began to roll down my cheeks. She took a deep breath and courageously lifted her gaze back to meet mine.

"I have been physically abused."

We both took a large step forward.

The floodgates opened. I felt naked, exposed, and vulnerable. I wondered if the feeling was mutual. I had the desire to reach out and comfort her and close the gap between us. With our eyes locked on each other and tears running down our faces, we embraced and comforted one another for a brief moment. Then we both took a step back as the questions continued and the sniffles in the room got louder.

"I have been sexually molested."

With our red swollen eyes locked on each other, I could see Jill swallow hard as she took a large step forward. I wanted to step forward too, just to let her know she wasn't alone and to comfort her.

"I am not good enough."

We both took a large step forward, as did the rest of the world, it seemed. You could hear sniffling and crying as each couple danced to their own rhythm of their past traumas and beliefs.

At some point, the statements finally stopped, and the only noise left were the drums reverberating throughout the room, awakening us to the present moment. Another round of affirmations began, bringing us full circle.

"I am good enough."

"I am enough."

"I am loved."

"I am exactly where I'm supposed to be."

"I am deliberate and afraid of nothing."

"I am safe."

"I am lovable."

"I am beautiful."

"I am capable."

"I find strength in my past."

"I am successful."

Afterward, I could immediately feel a healing of some of the old wounds I was still carrying. Among the many lessons I learned that weekend, I finally understood why the eyes are called "the windows to the soul." As Jill and I stared at each other deeply, our eyes boring into each other's souls, I felt as though I knew her and that she knew me, perhaps better than even some of my lifelong friends.

I was ashamed that I judged Jill's book by her cover. Although she and I appeared to be vastly different upon first blush, just beneath the surface, we were more the same than we knew, roots of the same sequoia trees inter-twined beneath the earth, spreading a hundred miles apart. We are all con-nected to each other and woven together by the same tapestry of mankind. We need each other to survive and grow to our fullest potential and, at times, confront our deepest pains to heal from them.

And so, while I tell my boys the importance of decorating their own personal book covers in the professional world, I also warn them that some of the best books are overlooked because they lack a good cover. People are not always who we think they are, and if we are willing to look below the surface and let go of our preconceived judgments, we may find some best sellers.

My goal is to help you find what resonates and feels good to you while giving you the fundamental styling parameters to look sharp and ultra-chic, no matter what profession you're in. This chapter is meant to be a jumping-off point for your own inspiration, and I encourage you to add your own uniqueness and flare. And of course, *own it*! This is your cover, after all.

CHAPTER 10

Olive Oyl:
Love the Skin You're In!

"You have been criticizing yourself for years, and it hasn't worked.
Try approving of yourself and see what happens."

—LOUISE HAY

If you want to look ten to fifteen pounds thinner without having to diet or go to the gym, then this chapter is for you. I am the queen of camouflage, and there are certainly plenty of tricks and styling techniques that can enhance your unique body shape.

One of the most common things I hear from someone who is potentially interested in my services is that they will reach out to me "when they have lost some weight."

Eventually, I get the call and hear a frustrated voice on the other end of the phone: "Jen, I think I need to just bite the bullet and hire you. I'm so tired of wearing the same four black things in my wardrobe, and I just don't know what to wear anymore."

I am personally thrilled and excited when I get this call because I know what lies ahead for them: a newfound confidence and joy in getting ready and stepping out into the world. I know that once they take the plunge with me that we are about to embark on a wonderful journey together. Watching the transformation of both the inner and the outer is remarkable, and the reason that I love what I do.

Still, weight seems to be the biggest deterrent for some when it comes to investing money into their wardrobes. And I get it. It's because people don't want to invest money into themselves until they are at their ideal weight. While I completely understand this logic, I don't agree with it for several reasons. First, the message that you are sending to yourself is that you're not worth investing in the way that you currently are. Second, this goes against the entire psychological phenomenon upon which this book is based, known as "enclothed cognition," and that the clothes we wear affect our behavior, attitudes, personality, mood, confidence, and the way we interact with others.

The first tip I have is about not only dressing for, but embracing your size. I had a client, Liz, who finally hired me after interviewing me multiple times over the course of two years. I thought about her often and hoped she would one day call because I knew I could help her. She did not know how to dress for her body type, often wearing oversize clothes to hide her shape, only making her look larger. This is a common mistake.

So, rule number one: if you want to look slimmer, wear more *fitted* clothing. I know this sounds counterintuitive, so I encourage you to test it out for yourself. Take a photo of yourself wearing something oversize in which you are hiding your body and then take a picture of yourself wearing something more fitting. The key is to figure out what fit is more flattering for your body and what makes you feel comfortable at the same time. This is exactly what happened to Liz. When Liz saw a picture of herself wearing what she thought worked for her, she was mortified at the image: she looked shapeless and at least ten pounds heavier. She realized that she didn't know what clothes would work best for her new body.

"Jen, it's Liz. I'm ready," she told me one day over the phone, sounding hopeless and frustrated. When I went to her house for the first time, she opened up to me about how she went from a size two to a size ten. The weight gain was taking a serious toll on her social life, her self-esteem, her sex life, and her marriage. Self-image is important because how we think about ourselves affects how we feel about ourselves and how we interact with others. Liz would dread the process of getting ready, trying to decide what to wear; she actually started turning down invitations and began isolating. She withdrew from her husband and her friendships. It sounded like she called me at exactly the right time in her life.

The first thing we did was to take inventory of what she needed and purge the clothes that weren't serving her anymore. She admitted that she kept her old clothes and even continued purchasing items that were several sizes smaller because she thought it would give her motivation to lose weight, but ironically, it was having the opposite effect. Liz would get depressed and anxious when she saw the smaller sized clothes sitting in her closet, so we removed those to make room for the new. By getting rid of what wasn't working for her anymore, she could create space physically and mentally for the clothes that would bring her joy, confidence, and happiness *now*. This wasn't an easy process for her; she wasn't ready to let go of the idea that she may not ever be a size two or four again. So, we decided on a realistic time frame for her to lose the weight, dated the box, stored the clothes, and labeled the box: FUTURE WARDROBE.

I want to make it clear I'm not a fan of "future shopping," and it's taken me a long time to be here now and not "future trip." "Future tripping" is also referred to as *anticipatory anxiety* and is a concept related to projecting into the future rather than living in the present.

When I first gave up smoking, I remember telling a close friend that I was petrified of being in Italy and Paris. I told her I couldn't imagine myself strolling the streets of Paris and not stopping in a café to enjoy a sauvignon blanc and a cigarette, or how I would be able to enjoy true Italian food in Florence without a cigarette and a glass of Sangiovese. I would envision this and panic.

Then she said, "Jen, when are you going?"

I paused and replied, "I don't know, but one day I will." I had nothing on the calendar and yet, this took up so much space in my head.

I have also been guilty of "future shopping," or buying clothes for future events that are not yet on the calendar. I was convinced I needed to look like the fashion influencer that I thought I was while I was traveling the world and documenting every detail of what I thought others wanted to see because I was a stylist. Never mind the fact that everyone and their mothers are now influencers, right?

I have gorgeous Zimmermann off-the-shoulder maxis, cover-ups with matching swimsuits for Greece, silk kaftans with bold statement necklaces and jeweled sandals for Morocco, safari Khakis with a stylish bush vest and expedition hat for my trip to Africa—all of which have been hanging in my closet for *years*.

Here's the reality: I have no trips planned. My weight fluctuates. I'm not a blogger or an influencer, whose lives are heavily edited and filtered. So, I encourage my clients to take the advice of Ram Dass: *Be here now.* Don't buy things for when you *eventually* lose ten pounds or for when you take that fabulous trip to the Bahamas. Strategically obtain things that serve you *now*—not six months or a year from now.

And speaking of clothes hanging in your closet, let me address those of you who have numerous garments hanging in your closets with the tags still attached. In my professional opinion, there are several reasons for this. First, you are purchasing items that you want to wear but are afraid to take the risk of stepping outside your box. So, when you tend to get ready, you gravitate toward what feels safe, rather than trusting you've picked a great fashion piece. Second, you love the item so much that you are afraid you might ruin it by wearing it. Last, you don't want to waste the item on just any ordinary event, so you're saving it for the *perfect* time or event to showcase it.

Here's my recommendation: Don't treat your clothes like your fine china or an expensive bottle of wine. Rather than waiting for the perfect occasion, surround yourself in beauty now, because you deserve it and life is unpredictable. Otherwise, the occasion might pass you by, or that item might just end up going out of style.

The next thing I did for Liz was to bring her a rack of clothes that would suit her personal silhouettes and overall lifestyle. Remember, not every trend is meant for everyone. I chose clothes that camouflaged the areas she was least comfortable with while accentuating her best assets. She learned what the best cuts were for her body type, how to use layering to trick the eye, monochromatic looks for a slimming effect, and how to use accessories. When she realized how simple it was to "up" her personal style, her confidence and self-esteem began to flourish, and she immediately started getting daily compliments on her style. In case you're wondering, she looked best in palazzo pants with light fabrics, loose shells, and dusters. Outerwear with different layers worked nicely, as well as longer outerwear pieces with shorter tops and shorter cardigans with tunics left out. She also looked good in fitted, long-sleeve dresses with ruche in the center. Wrap-style tops were flattering, and of course we got her a good support bra.

The influx of positive energy motivated her to exercise more and eat healthier. This prompted her to lose more weight, and by the time I visited her again several months later, she had dropped a few dress sizes. While she wasn't yet a size two, Liz's new positive self-image boosted her confidence and emotional well-being so much that she wasn't solely focused on the number on the scale and isolating herself anymore.

A wardrobe refresh is just one stop on the journey to a healthy life. We all know that there's deeper work to be done here to truly accept oneself and be happy on the inside. Fashion is just one tool that I've seen work in building self-confidence and self-esteem. And while some may argue that clothes are materialistic, I would argue that denying the significance or the value of the tangible things we put on our bodies doesn't honor its rightful place in the process of personal transformation.

In the past, I have struggled with my own personal beliefs about my weight and how they connect to self-esteem. The belief was simple: If I was ten pounds thinner, I was more desirable and lovable, and when I was ten pounds *heavier*, I was undesirable and unattractive. I had an unhealthy image of myself. As a result, I developed an unhealthy barometer when it came to measuring my weight in relation to my self-worth. My mental file cabinet needed some serious cleaning. It took some good therapy and a voluptuous pole dancer to teach me how to embrace my body and love myself just the way I am. (But more on that later.)

This belief began a long time ago. As a young child and a teenager, I was skin and bones and very self-conscious of my body. I couldn't wait to add a few pounds and develop some curves. Tia enjoyed teasing me and would call me Olive Oyl, Popeye's bony girlfriend. I hated that. I remember sitting on the toilet, thinking I couldn't wait for my thighs to be able to touch together. In my late teens and young adulthood, I started to blossom. My looks were starting to have value, a belief only reinforced by my father.

In high school, I would complain about my curve-less frame. I remember my father saying, "Jenny, you're beautiful just the way you are. I promise you that all the girls with the boobs and the perfect bodies will all be fat by the time they are twenty-five."

In turn, my young self interpreted that to mean I would be more lovable to men if I remained skinny and didn't gain weight. During my engagement, he only strengthened this belief further, reminding me not to gain weight after I became a wife.

"Jenny, don't ever let yourself go after you get married. Always take the time to put yourself together and look your best," he would say. "Your mother really let herself go. She was a size two when I married her and went to a size ten. It's just not fair to do that to your marriage." What he didn't mention was that what's also "unfair" to a marriage is if a husband is a serial cheater. Somehow, he forgot that part.

Sadly, my father valued women for their appearances and youthfulness, and these misguided values he felt, nevertheless, were important to pass on to me. Another vivid memory that played into this belief about having to look "perfect" occurred one summer day when I was twenty years old. I remember feeling excited to pick up my father and take him out to lunch. I showed up with the new Mazda Miata I had bought for myself, and I was wearing a pair of cutoff jean shorts. I remember being excited to tell him about my job promotion and how well I was doing at work. After he got into the car, I immediately started telling him about my new office and how my income was growing from the new account I had accumulated. I was really proud of myself. While I went on about my professional accomplishments, something that I wanted to be valued for, I noticed his eyes looking down at my legs. He cut me off mid-sentence, reached across the seat, squeezed my outer thigh, and said, "Be careful, baby, you're putting on a little weight."

I didn't know how to respond. I was so confused and hurt. I, in pursuing my career, hadn't noticed that I had put on any weight. Also, I was 5'5" and probably around 120 pounds, hardly overweight by any stretch of the imagination. It was a preposterous statement, but I didn't realize it then.

I went out and bought myself a scale, which would quickly become my daily friend or foe. I began noticing that a good portion of my happiness and self-worth was becoming more and more directly proportionate to my weight. The better my body, the more confident and sexier I felt, the more attention I would get, the more I felt valued and loved. Until one day, in my thirties, another belief started to surface: I was no longer attractive.

Again, this stemmed from my dad. In high school, I had tried to set him up with my friend's mother. When I asked him if he wanted to meet her, he said, "How old is she? If she's over thirty, then I'm not interested."

When pressed, he replied, "I don't find women over thirty attractive."

So, sometime in *my* thirties, I stopped feeling sexually attractive and completely felt like I lost my mojo. One afternoon, while my son was napping, I turned on the *Oprah Winfrey Show* where actress and writer Sheila Kelley was a guest. The main character of her latest film, which Sheila also starred in, happened to be a stripper. She learned how to pole dance for the role, taking lessons, which, she said, triggered something in her.

An erotic creature was awakened, giving her more confidence in her body. Her marriage improved, she became a happier mother, and she felt more complete. Pole dancing infused her daily life with some sexiness. After her role in the film and experiencing her own mental transformation through erotic dance, she opened up her own pole-dancing studio called S Factor, which she claimed "opens and strengthens the feminine body but also reconnects her to her vitality, sensuality, and her core desires." And that was all I needed to hear. That night at dinner, as my husband took a bite of chicken stir-fry, I announced that I was going to learn how to pole dance. Of course, he was shocked that the mother of his children was interested in the kinda-sorta thing strippers do. But after explaining what I had seen on Oprah, he needed no convincing that this would be a win-win for both of us. I signed up for my first S Factor class the following weekend. I left the baby boys with their dad on a Saturday afternoon and drove an hour to the city to reclaim my female sexual desire.

I checked in at the desk, walked into a dimly lit room with several poles attached from floor to ceiling, and grabbed a mat to sit down on, cross-legged, among the other ten or so nervous and embarrassed women, of all ages and sizes. The music was sensual, and candles flickered about the room, which had a sweet scent of vanilla in the air.

Then our teacher walked into the room, not looking at all what I had expected: She was a full-figured, voluptuous woman. Her hair tied up in a bun, she wore a pair of heavy-rimmed glasses, thick sweatpants, and a simple T-shirt.

How is she going to teach me *how to be sexy?* I thought. *Maybe this was a waste of time and money.*

I could not have been more wrong.

"Hi, my name is Bianca, and I want to welcome you to level one of S Factor. We will be learning several basic tricks and movements each week that will be choreographed, and at the end of level one, we will have put together your first dance routine," she said. "If it's okay with everyone, I would like to demonstrate the routine for you."

Bianca stood up and took her hair out of her bun. Her long, silky, shiny black hair cascaded down her back. She removed her glasses and slipped off her thick sweatpants and oversize T-shirt, revealing shiny metallic boy shorts and a lace push-up bra. Bianca stood securely in her own skin and exuded more confidence than anyone I had ever seen. As the music started, I watched her as she gracefully started moving her body with such fluidity, flexibility, and sensuality as she effortlessly lifted herself around the pole and glided gracefully onto the floor. I watched in amazement as she defied gravity and slithered around the room. I was astounded as she used her sexual expression to command the attention of everyone before her. She was not only confident in her own skin, but also fiercely—unapologetically, even—feminine.

I'm pretty sure my chin hit the floor; I was so in awe of Bianca—not just of the way she moved and danced, but also of how comfortable she was in her own body, the way she was erotic and commanding at the same time. At that moment, she was the sexiest woman I had ever seen, and I wanted to be just like her.

So, week after week, the ten of us would slowly let our guards down and "strip" away our insecurities and judgments. Bianca became our role model, guiding us toward finding or reigniting our femininity and embracing our bodies and sensuality. Bianca and I became friends, and I shared my insecurities, something that felt freeing. And in that freedom, I released any notions of fear I initially had.

Watching Bianca and the other ladies let their inner goddesses out, I learned that being sexy has nothing to do with your body or your weight. Practicing pole, along with some good therapy, taught me to love myself right where I am. I *am* beautiful and worthy of love, at any age or size. I learned to love the skin I was in, and pole dancing was the pathway to acceptance and reigniting that fire inside me. It took just a short time before I got my mojo back and threw away the scale. I haven't weighed myself since.

I'm not going to lie, I still feel better in my clothes when I'm thinner, and I might feel tempted to dim the lights a bit if I've gained a few pounds, but I know now that I'm loved and accepted just the way I am. And I really always was. Now, let's discuss the four body types and some stylist slimming tricks!

Grab your phone and hit the QR code *now*. I will discuss the four body types and detail what works best for *your* body shape. I will also teach you some styling tricks on how to look slimmer.

Fashion Tricks and Tips

to Flatter *Your* Body Type

When finding the most figure-flattering cuts, there are a few basic rules that you'll need to know. First, do not fixate on the size on the tag; you only limit yourself in doing so. Remember: All clothing is cut *differently*, and some brands and designers use different measurements. A size ten in Banana Republic certainly isn't the same as a size ten in Gucci, and that's perfectly okay! Just like age, size is just a number.

Second, we might both be a size twelve, but our body composition and proportions could be completely different. An apple-shaped and a pear-shaped size twelve might not fit the same-sized dress. I personally have to go up a size, sometimes two, and have my clothes altered because I have a larger bust. In the end, though, the dress fits my body like a glove, and I don't have to squeeze into a smaller size. Besides, when was the last time someone asked to see what size your dress is?

Keep in mind that these are general guidelines and are not set in stone. For example, not all apple shapes have large breasts. Figuring out your body type and understanding how to dress for it can be a bit confusing; it takes some patience.

And I'm here to help! Below are general characteristics associated with different body shapes, as well as my list of styling tips. As is typical of fashion, there are no hard rules. I, personally, believe we can be a blend of two body types. These shapes also apply to plus sizes. Plus-size model Ashley Graham is an hourglass shape, while Fluvia Lacerda is a pear.

Now that you know to treat size as just another number, here are my top ten styling tips for looking your most flattering in clothes:

1: Monochromatic Dressing

Black is a no-brainer. Everyone knows that the number one way to look thinner is to wear *all black*, but that can also become very boring. Try monochromatic dressing with a different color instead; simply wear one color head-to-toe to create a long, lean silhouette. Think all burgundy, gray, navy, or even a bold red. Dressing monochromatically has a slimming effect because it creates a vertical line that lengthens your body and can help accentuate your height.

2: Maximize Your Assets

You can do this by highlighting the smallest area of your body. For example, if you have an hourglass figure, pick pieces that cinch your waist for a dramatic effect. If you are apple-shaped and have great legs, try an A-line minidress with tights and booties.

3: Undergarments

The right undergarments can make or break an outfit, so be sure you have the right ones. (See Chapter 10, titled "Fashion Foreplay: What's Underneath Matters Too.")

4: Perfect Prints

Stick to small-scale prints rather than big bold ones. Vertical stripes only!

5: Layer

Outerwear is your friend. Try a duster worn open over a monochromatic look, or an open outerwear blazer or jacket that doesn't hit at the widest part of your body. Play with dimensions by wearing a cropped jacket with a longer layered shirt underneath.

6: Details

Look for clothes that have built-in vertical paneling details. This will help create the illusion of a smaller frame.

7: Neck and Neck

V-neck and scoop-neck cuts help elongate your neck if you feel the need to.

8: In the Jeans

High-rise and bootcut jeans are your best friends for creating an hourglass shape and a smaller waist.

9: Well-Heeled

Pointy-toed shoes and high heels elongate the legs.

10: Fake It

If your skin tone is pale and you're not blessed with black, brown, or tan skin, a fake tan has a slimming effect.

Body Types

FRIENDS AND FOES

Hourglass

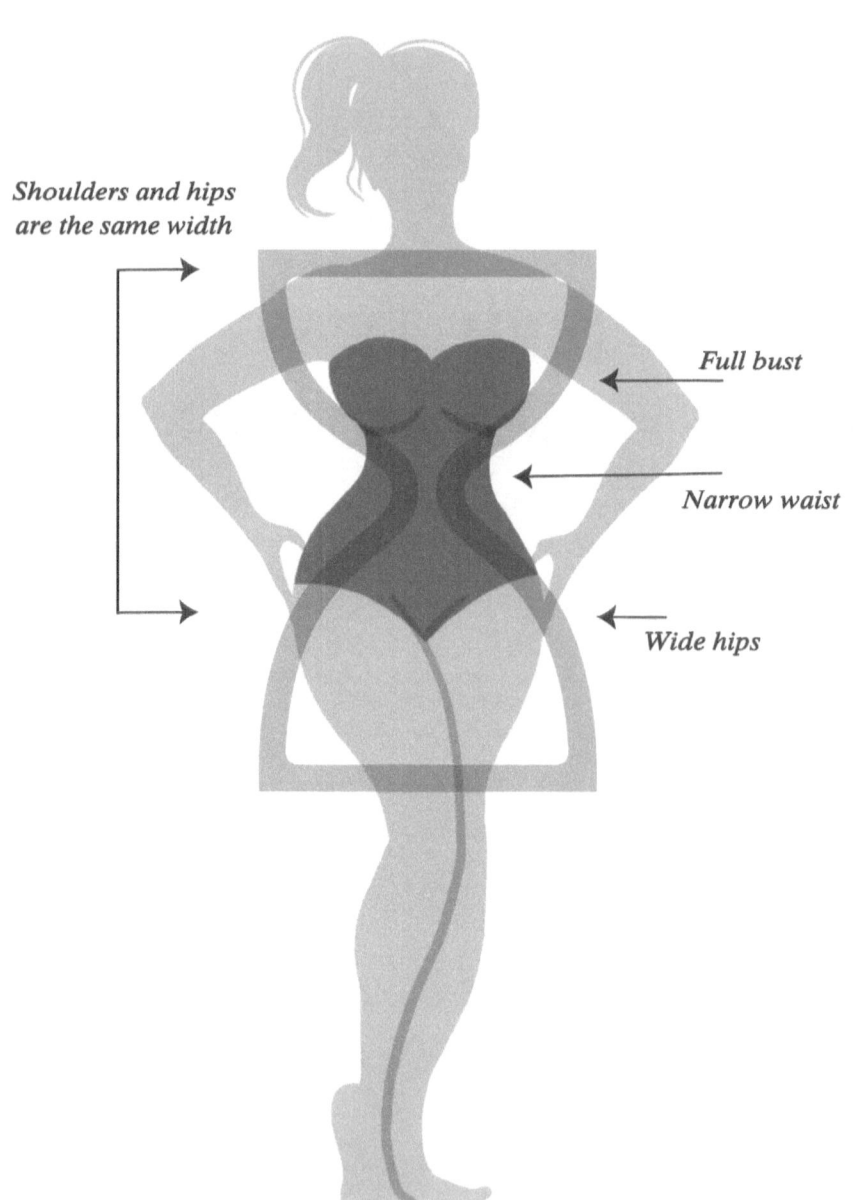

Shoulders and hips are the same width

Full bust

Narrow waist

Wide hips

The Hourglass Shape

The hourglass shape is defined by a woman's body measurements—the circumference of the bust, waist, and hips. Hourglass body shapes have a wide bust, a narrow waist, and wide hips with shoulders and hips being roughly the same width. You tend to have a short waist and round bottom. Think of the iconic Marilyn Monroe, who was known to be a size fourteen (which would be a size eight to ten today) with measurements of 35"-22"-35". Some people describe the hourglass shape as "curvy with a well-defined waist." It's all about celebrating your waist and showing off your neckline. Focus on silhouettes that draw the eye to the slenderest part of your body. Famous hourglass shapes include Sophia Loren, Beyoncé, and Jennifer Lopez.

THE HOURGLASS SHAPE

STYLING TIPS	
• Embrace the bum • Define your waist • Show off your curves	• Pick stretchy fabrics • Avoid anything shapeless and boxy
Tops (Friend)	**Tops (Foe)**
• Fitted wrap tops • Fitted V-neck or boat neck • Form-fitting jersey knits • Peplums, as these tops mirror your shape • Button-down with sleeves rolled up to where the waist hits	• Tunic tops (they typically stop right at the waistline) • Empire tops • Turtlenecks (they create an area around the bustline so that it appears larger) • High-neck tops (high necklines can make the chest look even fuller) • Kimono tops • Tube tops
Outerwear (Friend)	**Outerwear (Foe)**
• Trench coats, belts • Fitted blazers that cinch at the waist and flare at the hip	• Boxy jackets
Dresses and Skirts (Friend)	**Dresses and Skirts (Foe)**
• Wrap dresses are your best friends • Fit-and-flare dresses • Body-con dresses with stretchy fabrics • High-waisted and pencil skirts (they elongate the legs; add a flounce around the bottom to balance fuller tops and jackets)	• Loose, free-flowing fabrics • A-line dresses • Empire-waisted dresses • Baby doll dresses

THE HOURGLASS SHAPE

Pants and Jumpsuits (Friend)	Pants and Jumpsuits (Foe)
• High-waisted and narrow-waisted flared jeans or trousers (they balance out the hips and create the illusion of longer legs; flaring should start from top and not from the knee) • Boot-cut jeans • Fitted jumpsuits • Full-length, fitted skinny jeans and leggings • Pro tip: See a tailor to pinch in the waist of your pants	• Low-waisted pants (unless your stomach is very flat) • Cropped pants • Cargo pants with large pockets • Pockets that add weight to your hips
Accessories (Friend)	**Accessories (Foe)**
• Belts are your best friend!	• Lucky you, accessorize all you like. But keep it in proportion
Shoes (Friend)	**Shoes (Foe)**
• Closed-toe pumps • Nude pumps • Pointy-toed shoes	• Shoes with ankle straps
Proceed with Caution	
• Baggy clothes • Vertical stripes • Bold patterns	• Pants with large pockets on front or back • Heavy, thick fabric like corduroy, tweed, and wools • Skinny jeans (layer to camouflage with a duster or cardigan)

Triangle

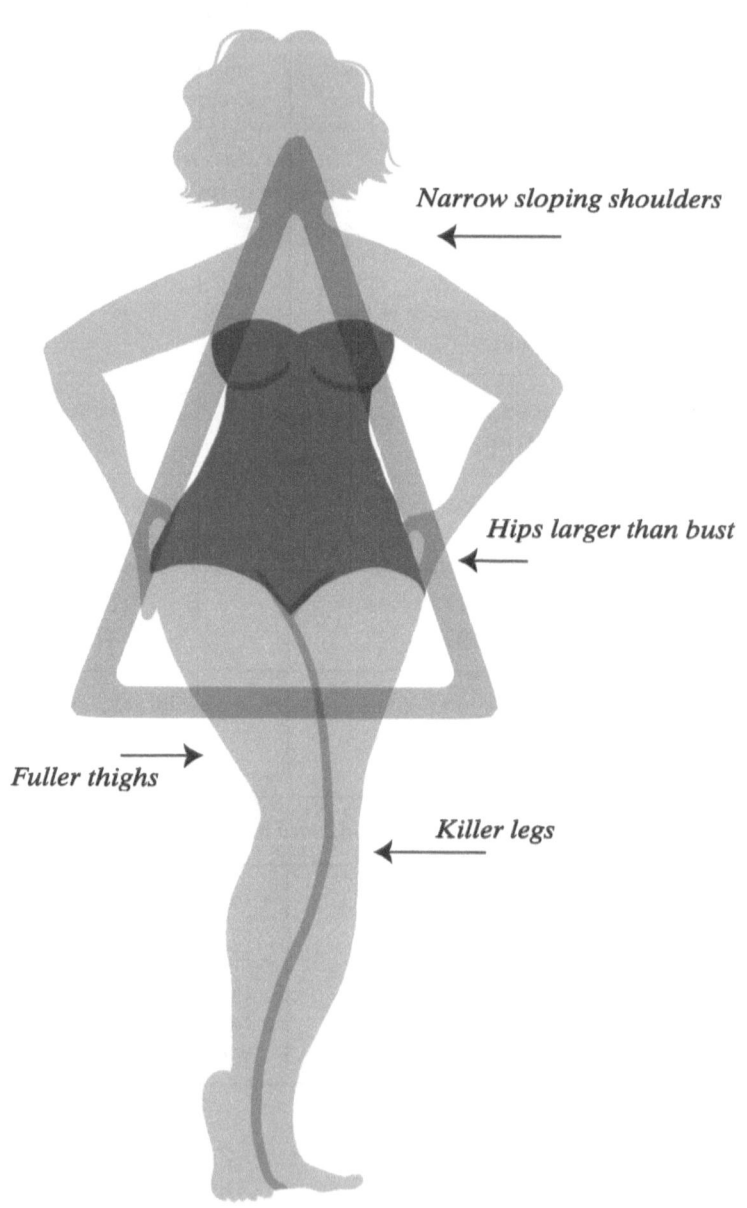

Narrow sloping shoulders ←

Hips larger than bust ←

→ *Fuller thighs*

Killer legs ←

The Pear Shape (or Triangle Shape)

The pear, also known as the "triangle" shape, has narrow or sloping shoulders, with hips that are larger than your bust and wider than your shoulders. You may have a round bottom, fuller thighs, and slender lower legs. The key here is to elongate your figure so that you look less bottom-heavy by drawing attention to your upper body. In the pear club: Kelly (Clarkson) Brianne, Kate Winslet, and Rihanna.

THE PEAR SHAPE

STYLING TIPS	
• Always wear a solid or dark color on the bottom • Try bright colors or bold patterns on top • A statement necklace draws the attention upward • Never tuck in your tops	• Avoid drawing attention to your hips • Outerwear should hit above or below the hips • Horizontal stripes on top create a balancing effect
Tops (Friend)	**Tops (Foe)**
• Button-down shirts • Tunic tops (as long as they don't cling to your belly) • Halter tops • Strapless clothes • Bright colors and patterns (this will draw attention to your upper body) • Puffed or flutter sleeves • Embellished shirts with interesting collars • Cowl necks • Tops with shoulder pads	• Kimono tops • Peplum tops
Outerwear (Friend)	**Outerwear (Foe)**
• Cropped jackets with upper detailed embellishments (wear a longer, loose-fitting top underneath—longer than the jacket—that hits below the hips) • Sweaters or cardigans that hit below or above the hips • Dusters • Longer jackets that are nipped in at the waist • Sweaters or jackets that hit at your widest point • Wide belts (instead, use a thin belt, worn slightly higher than your waistline in the same color as your pants or dress)	• Peplum-style coats, as they emphasize the hips • Straight-cut and boxy coats

THE PEAR SHAPE

Dresses and Skirts (Friend)	Dresses and Skirts (Foe)
• A-line skirts and dresses • Fit-and-flare dresses • Tulip dresses • Wrap dresses • Off-the-shoulder, fit-and-flare cuts • Strapless dresses with full skirts	• Drop-waist dresses • Miniskirts (they highlight the heaviest areas) • Pencil skirt • Shift dresses • Sheath dresses • Body-con dresses (unless off-the-shoulder or has ruche)
Pants and Jumpsuits (Friend)	**Pants and Jumpsuits (Foe)**
• Flat-front slacks or jeans • Tailored straight-leg pants (avoid side pockets) • Flared jeans or pants (this draws the eye away from the hips) • Boot-cut jeans or pants • Palazzo pants with a well-defined waistband • High-waisted pants	• Skinny jeans or cigarette pants (if you wear either, pair with a long top that goes over your hips and an outerwear piece) • Pants that add weight to hips • Patterned pants
Accessories (Friend)	**Accessories (Foe)**
• Accessories are your best friend. They draw the attention away from the hips • Scarves • Statement necklaces • Statement earrings • Brooches on lapels	• Be cautious of belts—keep them thin and high
Shoes (Friend)	**Shoes (Foe)**
• Knee-length boots • Pointy-toed heels, especially nude ones that will make your legs look longer	• Round-toed shoes • Ankle boots • Shoes with ankle straps (but avoid shoes that cut off at the ankle, like booties; they shorten your legs)
Proceed with Caution	
• White jeans can be tricky and appear to make you look heavier—camouflage your hips with a layered, mid-thigh outerwear piece, like a cardigan	• Avoid a wide belt; a thin belt will help define your waistline

Inverted Triangle

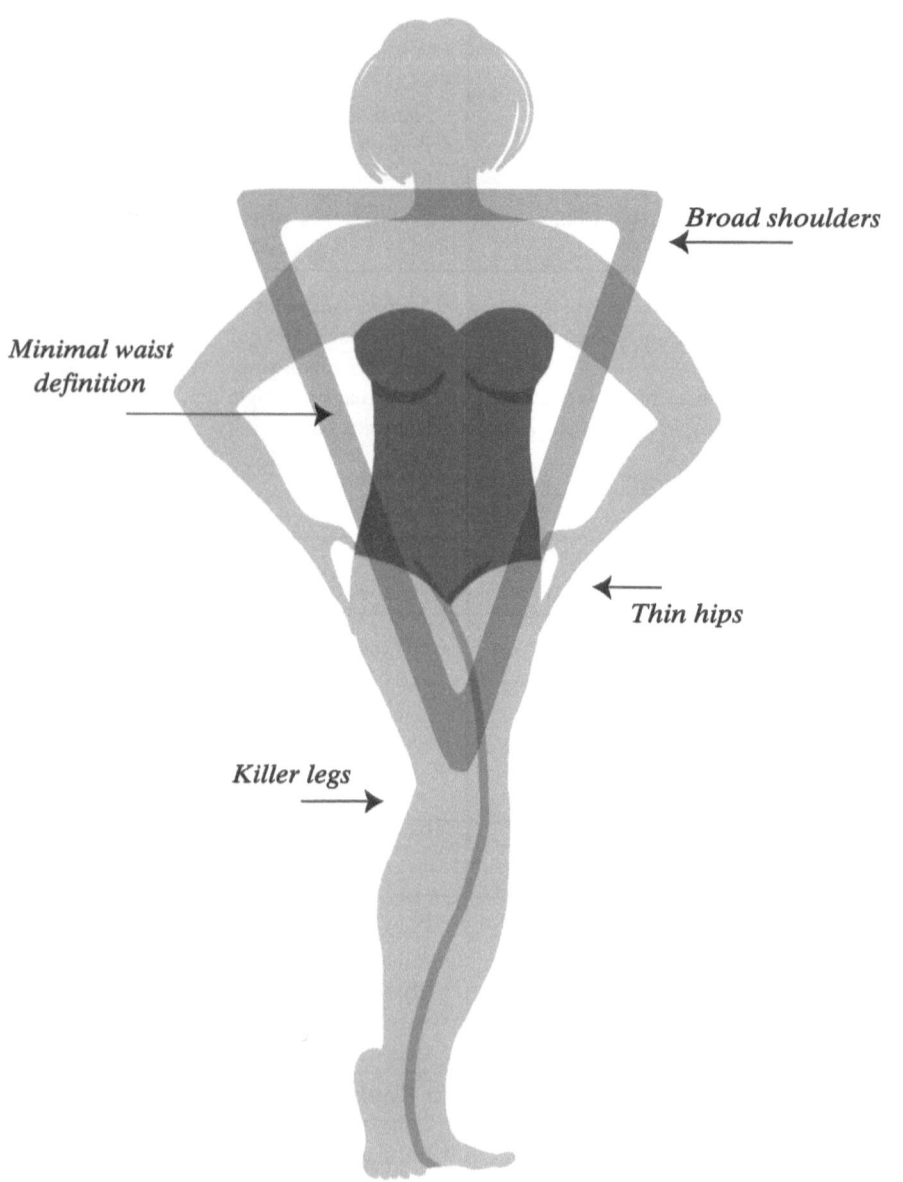

Broad shoulders

Minimal waist definition

Thin hips

Killer legs

The Inverted Triangle Shape

The inverted triangle can sometimes be confused with the apple shape. The distinguishing characteristics are broad shoulders and thin hips with no waist definition. Both body shapes may have a larger bust with killer legs. A well-toned inverted triangle is one of the most coveted body types. But it's all about balancing the upper and lower body so that "triangles" don't look top heavy or too broad. The trick is to minimize the attention to your chest and shoulders and add volume to your lower half to harmonize your silhouette. In the inverted triangle club: Cindy Crawford, Renée Zellweger, and Demi Moore.

THE INVERTED TRIANGLE SHAPE

STYLING TIPS	
• Embrace your strong shoulders (they help to create the illusion of a very small waistline) • Show off those legs! • Wear darker colors on top and lighter colors on bottom	• Keep jewelry small on the upper half of your body to avoid drawing attention to your shoulders • Avoid shoulder pads and puffed sleeves at all costs • Keep it simple and steer clear of tops with embellishments
Tops (Friend)	**Tops (Foe)**
• Wrap tops • Halter tops • Crew and scoop necks • Tailored tops that tie or nip at the waist • Peplums • Asymmetrical cuts • Kimono and dolman-sleeve tops	• Tops with shoulder pads or flutter sleeves • Wide or plunging necklines • Spaghetti-strap tops (look for ones with slightly thicker straps) • Wide, off-the-shoulder tops • Loud patterns • Billowing, shapeless blouses • Fitted long sleeves
Outerwear (Friend)	**Outerwear (Foe)**
• Nipped or belted at the waist • Straight and deconstructed cuts • Peplums • Jackets that extend beyond the hips • Sweaters or jackets with hip details • Wrap cardigans	• Double-breasted • Big collared jackets or coats with shoulder details • Jackets with shoulder pads
Dresses and Skirts (Friend)	**Dresses and Skirts (Foe)**
• Maxi and midi skirts that create volume • Tulip, box pleat, and A-line skirts • Dresses with paneled or nipped waists • Tiered, full, and pleated skirts • Shift, A-line, and pleated dresses	• Tight, fitted dresses that don't add volume to the hips • Watch necklines and avoid embellishments that emphasize the upper body

THE INVERTED TRIANGLE SHAPE

Pants and Jumpsuits (Friend)	Pants and Jumpsuits (Foe)
• Palazzo pants • Baggy, boyfriend, and boot-cut jeans • Boot-cut flare jeans or trousers • Flare and wide trousers	• Skinny-fit jeans
Accessories (Friend)	**Accessories (Foe)**
• Large bangles and cocktail rings • Long pendant necklaces	• Large earrings and statement necklaces
Shoes (Friend)	**Shoes (Foe)**
• Go for bold, bright, and eye-catching shoes • Wedges and block heels	• If you are petite, avoid shoes that cut off your legs
Proceed with Caution	
• Wide necklines • Clothing that is too fitted may create a muscular build	

Apple

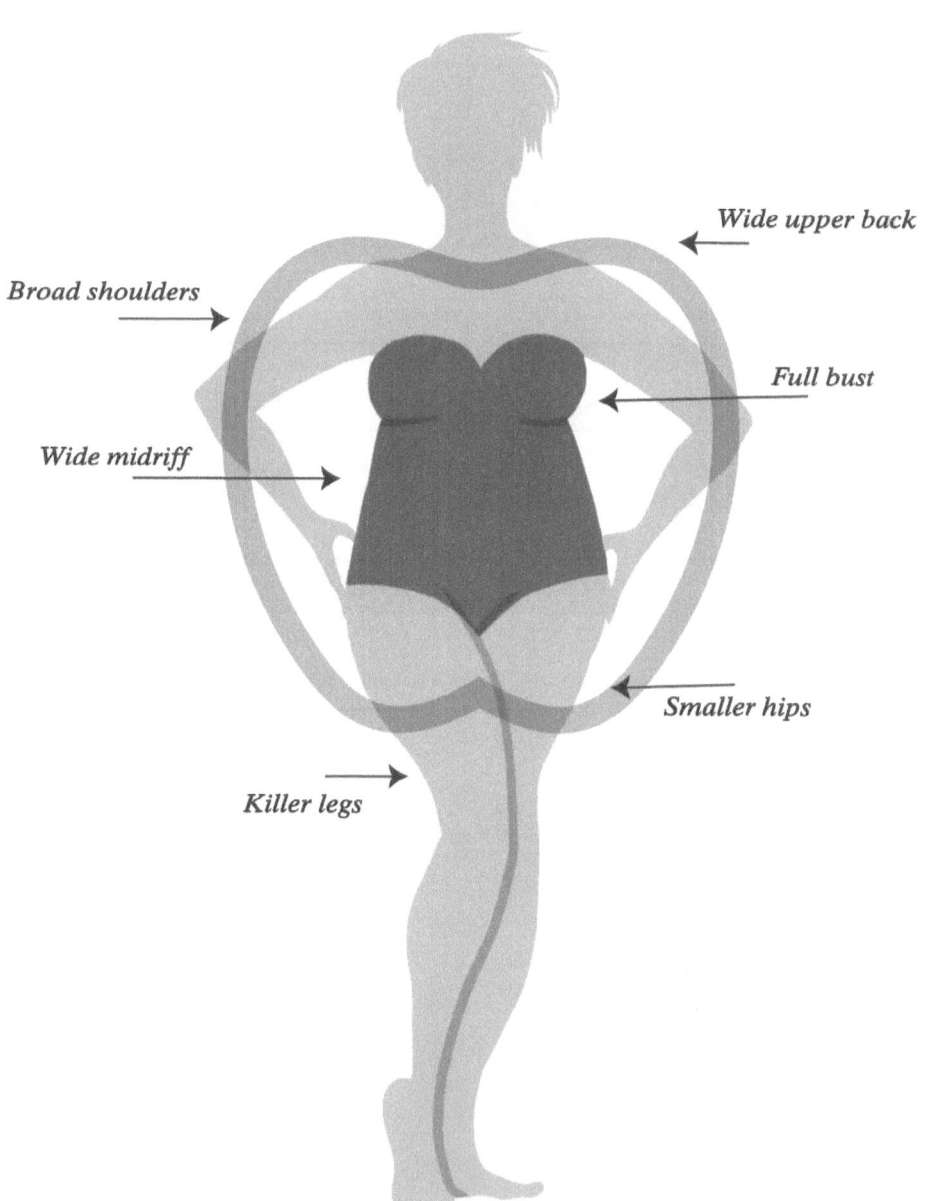

Wide upper back

Broad shoulders

Full bust

Wide midriff

Smaller hips

Killer legs

The Apple Shape

The apple shape is described as "top heavy," meaning your weight leans more toward your upper body. Apples have a wide torso, broad shoulders, and full bust, waist, and upper back. Apple-shaped bodies tend to have thinner arms, legs, and hips and tend to gain weight in their waistlines. The key here is to balance it out, draw the attention away from your belly, and emphasize your legs. Being an apple shape does not mean that you are heavy. You can be tall and slim and still have an apple-shaped body. In the club: Jennifer Hudson and Catherine Zeta-Jones.

THE APPLE SHAPE

STYLING TIPS	
• If you have great legs, flaunt them • For more leg coverage, try opaque tights or nylons • Don't cover up your body with loose, shapeless clothing • Define your curves • A well-fitted bra is a must	• Avoid unnecessary bulk around your middle by choosing soft fabric • Draw attention to legs and shoulders • Look for clothing with vertical lines to create a long and lean silhouette • Emphasize your cleavage to draw attention upward • Ruche is your best friend
Tops (Friend)	**Tops (Foe)**
• Wrap tops (they will create a more defined waistline and show off your bust) • Dolman sleeves • Empire-waist cuts (they draw attention to the slimmest point of your body) • Loose, V-neck blouses • Peplums (this creates the illusion of an hourglass and covers your midsection) • Asymmetrical tops (this helps create slimming lines) • Patterns can create a camouflage effect	• Fitted tops • High necklines • Tight, clingy T-shirts • Voluminous, shapeless tops • Decorative necklines (this causes the eye to be drawn upward)
Outerwear (Friend)	**Outerwear (Foe)**
• Open-front jackets without closures • Cardigans without closures • Long sweater vests • Dusters • Long lapel blazers	• Big puffy jackets • Shapeless, boxy garments

THE APPLE SHAPE

Dresses and Skirts (Friend)	Dresses and Skirts (Foe)
• Empire waists • Shifts • Off-the-shoulder • Wrap dresses (ties on the side of the dress, not in the front) • Bias cuts (cut on a diagonal) with loose fabric • Dresses with ruche, draping, or layers • A-line and pencil skirts	• Tiered ruffle skirts • Body-con dresses and tops
Pants and Jumpsuits (Friend)	**Pants and Jumpsuits (Foe)**
• Leggings • Straight jeans • Skinny jeans • Trousers, flared or straight	• Wide-leg trousers
Accessories (Friend)	**Accessories (Foe)**
• Statement earrings, rings, cuffs • Long necklaces • Scarves	• Small petite bags, as they don't balance out the shape of your body
Shoes (Friend)	**Shoes (Foe)**
• Bold-colored shoes to show off your legs • Nude shoes to make legs look even longer • Embellished shoes • Pointy-toed shoes • Single-strap shoes • Over-the-knee boots • *Anything* that shows off those legs!	• Mid-calf ankle boots, as they can shorten your legs
Proceed with Caution	
• Beware of clingy materials, especially around the waistline. Belts are a good way to cinch the waist! However, make sure your belt is worn at the thinnest part of your midsection and that its color is the same as the garment's	• For outerwear, buttoning or closing is optional for the ones I suggested, so make fit the priority here. Choose sizes that fit your shoulders best. Fill in any "open" space with a scarf or a long necklace

Rectangle

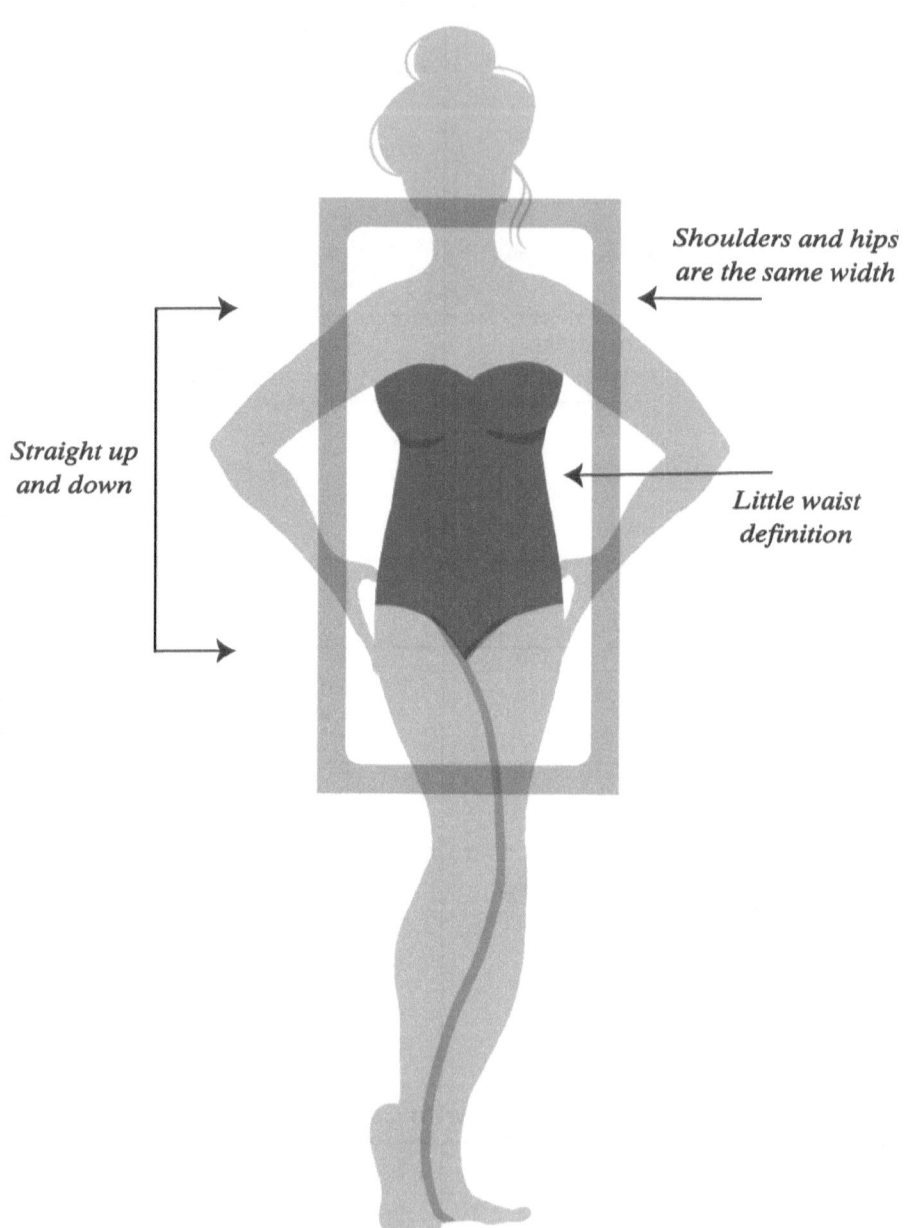

Shoulders and hips
are the same width

Straight up
and down

Little waist
definition

The Rectangle Shape (or Straight Shape)

The rectangle body type, also known as the "straight" or "athletic body type," has proportions that are very straight up and down. Your shoulders and hips will be roughly the same width, with little waist definition, regardless of whether you're a size four or size twenty-four. You may be described as more muscular than curvy. The goal for rectangle body types is to create curves for a more hourglass shape.

You can play up any part of your body. If you want to add some volume up top, try rocking a small shoulder pad or a flutter sleeve. Create more curves by cinching your waist with a high-waisted belt. If you are very small busted, invest in a good push-up bra. In the club: Natalie Portman, Gwyneth Paltrow, Gwen Stefani, and yours truly.

THE RECTANGLE SHAPE

STYLING TIPS	
• Play up your shoulders with a puff sleeve • Stay away from shapeless or boxy clothing • Define your waist	• Try a peplum to draw attention to your waist • Fill your hips with a wide-leg silhouette
Tops (Friend)	**Tops (Foe)**
• Embellishment around bust and shoulders • Halter tops • Off-the-shoulder • Button-down (tucked and belted) • Scoop necks and V-necks • Puffed and flutter sleeves • Sweetheart necklines • Peplums • Wrap tops • Princess sleeves	• Tunics • Boxy shapes • Bell sleeves
Outerwear (Friend)	**Outerwear (Foe)**
• Double-breasted coats or jackets • Belts • Peplums • Structured jackets • Fitted blazers • Coats that hit below the knees (this will elongate your frame) • Straight-cut coats • Dusters • Wraps	• Boxy jackets • Cropped jackets

THE RECTANGLE SHAPE

Dresses and Skirts (Friend)	Dresses and Skirts (Foe)
• Fit-and-flare • Peplum dresses • Body-con dresses • X-line dresses • U- and V-neckline dresses • Asymmetrical cuts • Wrap dresses	• Boxy shapes • Shift dresses or skirts
Pants and Jumpsuits (Friend)	**Pants and Jumpsuits (Foe)**
• Trousers • Flared trousers • Skinny jeans • High-waisted jeans or pants • Flare-cut jeans	• Shapeless, baggy pants • Palazzo pants
Accessories (Friend)	**Accessories (Foe)**
• When it comes to jewelry, anything goes • Belts are your best friend, but keep them thin and neutral to create a defined waist • Round clutches and bags that tuck under the arm work best • Statement earrings	• No foes here!
Shoes (Friend)	**Shoes (Foe)**
• Rectangles can rock all styles of shoes, but a good trick to feel less athletic is to try a ballerina slipper or a feminine T-strap. I personally am a rectangle and love a chunky men's-style loafer	• Be cautious of heavy, chunkier heels, as they can detract from your lean, long legs
Proceed with Caution	
• Be careful with long, layering necklaces. They can elongate your body	• Choose bags that aren't too oversize and rest at your waist

And there you have it! I hope that you now have a better understanding of the five different body types and that you can clearly identify your own. You also have knowledge of the most figure-flattering shapes and styles for your body. Head on over to my website by using the QR code for a free download of your personal body type shopping cheat sheet to take with you the next time you go!

CHAPTER 11

Fashion Foreplay— What's Underneath Matters Too

"Real elegance is everywhere, especially in the things that don't show."

—Christian Dior

This chapter is dedicated to anyone who feels as though they have lost their MOJO, or if you're thinking, *"My outer joy is off."* There will be a bit specifically for men in this chapter too. So, gentlemen, if you're reading this, get ready: you're about to get the *real scoop* on what most women think when it comes to men and fashion.

I am fascinated by the psychology behind what motivates people to hire me. Sartorial laziness is an easy habit to slip into and a common complaint I hear from spouses after being together for a long time. I also commonly get calls inquiring about my services from men and women who are newly divorced and on the dating circuit again. They tend to want to "up their game" and feel more confident while out in the dating world again. They also want to leave lasting impressions on the people they do go on dates with. But what really intrigues me is why it takes a divorce or a breakup for someone to want to put more energy and effort into their appearance, to "get their sexy back."

Another common request for my styling services is for what I like to refer to as "decade birthdays," those big milestone celebrations when someone turns thirty, forty, fifty, or sixty. These monumental birthdays trigger something that ignites the desire to look their absolute best on that special day. My clients know that even if we only *think* we look better, we feel better.

Have you ever had the experience of wearing something to an event or dinner party that made you feel like a million bucks? You walked into the room feeling secure and completely confident, and when you look back at the event, you can remember exactly what you were wearing and how it made you feel.

On the contrary, have you ever left the house feeling insecure about how you looked, and did it affect your overall mood? This is because how we present ourselves can change the quality of our experiences. I can take a trip down memory lane just by perusing my wardrobe. I still remember the first dress I wore on my first date with my husband and that coat that I haven't worn since my father's funeral.

According to a study published in *Social Psychological and Personality Science*, what we wear can make us feel more powerful and even think more clearly.[11] According to numerous studies, if it's a little dopamine you're looking for during depressing times, there's evidence to suggest that wearing bright colors and fun clothes can help lift your mood.

So, the good news is, if you're feeling like you need to boost your self-esteem, clothes are one simple tool to do that, almost instantaneously. And if you're single and wanting to invite some romance into your life or, for the coupled up, need to rekindle the flame with your significant other, you might consider ditching the granny panties and start with what's underneath.

No one knew this more than Florenz Ziegfeld Jr. He was the most important and influential producer in the history of Broadway musicals, a pioneer and creator of the "showgirl." The Ziegfeld Follies were a quartet of elaborately dressed, beautiful showgirls featured in theatrical productions on Broadway from 1907 to 1931. They danced in intricately choreographed synchronization and wore elaborate uniforms, hand-picked by Ziegfeld for each performance.

One of my favorite stories about Ziegfeld is about the petticoats he purchased in the early 1900s during the Great Depression. He would not

---

11 Matthew Hutson and Tori Rodriguez, "Dress for Success: How Clothes Influence Our Performance," Scientific American, January 1, 2016, https://www.scientificamerican.com /article/dress-for-success-how-clothes-influence-our-performance.

settle for anything but the very best, regardless of cost for his showgirls. They dressed in mink, satin, chinchilla, and lace. Ziegfeld purchased all the attire for the Follies dancers, each of whom wore a petticoat under their garments, never to be seen by viewers. At Ziegfeld's insistence, each petticoat was made of luxurious Irish linen.

While Ziegfeld's backers objected to the exorbitant costs of the petticoats, which were a small fortune at that time, claiming that nobody would see them and that they were a waste of money, he responded, "They will, and it does something to their walk."

Ziegfeld seemed to understand the connection between how we feel in clothing and how that plays out in our "performance," whether on the stage or in life. He knew that we carry ourselves differently when we dress ourselves in certain ways—even in ways that others might not see!

I believe this to be very true in my own experience, and I'd like to let you in on a little secret: I believe that the very first thing you put on—the garments or the fragrances that go on our naked bodies before we get dressed—can create a shift in our vibration. I learned about this mindset firsthand when I was a college student and just coming into my own feminine sexuality.

Finding a job in college proved to be very challenging, as I was struggling to afford to pay my rent. I was able to secure a job at a coffee shop a few days a week, where I would go to work at 5:00 A.M. before my classes started. But I was getting exhausted trying to keep up and I desperately wanted a different job. I picked up an extra shift from a coworker one morning and struck up a conversation with a customer I was waiting on.

I discovered she was a manager at Victoria's Secret at the local mall and had an opening in the beauty and bath department. The job didn't offer commissions, but the hours were much better. So, I decided to quit my waitressing job to sell body butters, soaps, and perfumes, in the hopes that I could eventually move on to selling lingerie and earn some commissions.

Shortly after I was hired, one of my managers said it was highly recommended that the employees wear Victoria's Secret undergarments beneath their clothing to work. I thought this was the most absurd and annoying request I had ever heard, especially since I was working in the bath depart-ment. This also posed a challenge because I could hardly afford my rent, and I wasn't even dating anyone who could appreciate pretty panties. However, I wanted to please my manager and work my way up in the company. So, when I got my first paycheck, I unenthusiastically purchased a satin-trim push-up bra, a lace bodysuit, and a few pairs of panties. Initially, I was annoyed and resentful.

This is ridiculous, I thought. *I'm wearing lingerie under my clothes that no one will see, that isn't particularly comfortable, and that I can't even afford. I mean, isn't lingerie something you wear to turn on your partner?* I didn't even have a boyfriend. But every few days, I would put on my new undergarments and, begrudgingly, head off to work.

But something very interesting started happening. Within just a short time, I noticed myself at the end of day taking my clothes off and staring at myself, in my lingerie, in the mirror. I mean, *really looking* at my unique self. I started noticing how beautiful lingerie is to look at and the way it's designed to accentuate the body and all its natural curves. The ribbons, the lace, and the satin all crafted to look and feel sensual.

I loved the way the lingerie lifted my breasts and hugged my feminine curves. I began to notice how feminine lingerie made me feel and, within that femininity, I also felt empowered.

One day while getting dressed, I felt an urge to turn on some music and move my body. I danced around my apartment in my lingerie, accessing a part of me that felt so alive, an act of self-love and appreciation for my sexuality. I felt in control, confident, and *seductive.* And that's when I had the epiphany that lingerie isn't for *him*; it's for *me.*

The next time I got dressed for work, I was no longer resentful but rather appreciative about this newfound sexual treasure and wanted to save a little money to buy a few more things. When I put on my lingerie, my energy shifted and I felt much more in tune with my sexual desires. I even began fantasizing about potential relationships and experiences I wanted to have. Just knowing that underneath my T-shirt and jeans was a lace bra and silk panties, or peeking out of my white button-down shirt was a feminine bodysuit was invigorating and powerful. I must have been exuding that energy because I noticed that I was attracting the attention of the men around me. Nothing had changed, and yet, *everything* had changed.

Today, I have been married twenty-six years, and lingerie still plays an important role in my life. I have a drawer full of all kinds of "play clothes." They make me feel powerful, feminine, and totally in control. Sometimes it's for him, and sometimes it's for me. One of our favorite things to do is to go lingerie shopping together, especially when we travel. Keeping your marriage alive takes effort, and using lingerie as foreplay is just one very easy tool to keep things spicy.

If you're not ready to wear lingerie yet, try sending a pair of panties and a bra to your significant other at the office or slipping a pair of your underwear (with a little bit of your signature perfume) into your significant other's briefcase or workbag.

If you're on your own and don't feel comfortable just wearing lingerie by itself, try wearing it under a trench coat, a duster, or a silk robe. Ask yourself these questions: *If I were with the person of my dreams, what would I choose for myself to wear? Would it be a little bit sexier than what I wear now? Would I put a little more effort into my dates?*

Victoria's Secret let me in on this *secret*: lingerie can evoke a new mindset and emotions, no matter what size you are; an idea also emphasized by Bianca from S Factor. Of course, comfort can be an issue, so I would suggest incorporating it, little by little, to add some romance into your life. I challenge you to take note of your mindset when you do. Don't wait for when you're dating or for a special occasion; adorn your body with a little leather, lace, or satin *now*. Allow yourself to explore your own sensuality and self-expression. Granny panties do nothing for the libido, and wearing something with a little more sex appeal sends a message to your brain (and the universe) that you are ready for something sexier in your life.

So, just as lingerie can be used for foreplay, most heterosexual women don't fantasize about their men wearing lingerie. However, we do have some definite things that turn us on and off. I once had a woman pull me aside and beg me to have a talk with her husband. She was willing to spend any amount of money to get him to care about his wardrobe and his appearance. He, of course, refused and referred to her as the "fashion police," not taking her requests seriously. Having had significant financial success throughout his career and now retired, he felt like he earned the right to wear whatever he felt like, with comfort being the priority. Unfortunately, his idea of comfort was turning her off. I'm all for comfort too, but there's a way to look handsome and comfortable without sacrificing style. On the next page, you'll find my top styling tips for men.

Men's Styling Tips

Tip #1:

Many women are turned on by men who look stylish and put together. For a woman, a well-dressed man is fashion foreplay. It's a turn-on! His idea of comfort might consist of oversize slogan T-shirts, baggy pants that desperately need hemming, mid-calf socks with Birkenstock sandals, and a fisherman's hat that has no business being worn outside of a fishing boat. I call this type of dresser "The Schlump."

Tip #2:

Women are not turned on by The Schlump, regardless of his status or financial success.

Tip #3:

Oversize, baggy slogan T-shirts are a turn-off, and sponsored event wear should only be worn to that sponsored event.

Tip #4:

Ditch the Birkenstocks or Crocs, as they are sexy to a very small population, if at all. Shoes are one of the first things that a woman notices on a man. It's because shoes tell a girl right away a few things about you. If your shoes look cheap or flimsy, she will suspect you're a cheapskate, and if they're worn down, she'll think you don't care about your appearance—so, what else do you neglect? Which leads me to . . .

Tip #5:

Invest in a few good pairs of stylish shoes (and take the tags off the bottom!). Trends change for sneakers, but the basic must-haves are: a Chelsea boot in black, a brown chukka boot, a loafer, clean low-top sneakers in black, gray, and white, and an oxford lace-up for dressier occasions.

Tip #6:

Man-scape. This may come as a shock, but most women do not like hair coming out of the nostrils or ears, bushy ungroomed eyebrows, or extremely hairy chests. I know you might think hair is a sign of masculinity, but generally, we would prefer a well-groomed man. Trim your hairy chests and privates, pluck your nose and ear hairs, and clean and trim your nails and toenails, especially if wearing flip-flops (which should only be worn on vacation or in a pool/ beach setting). And it's okay to get manicures. A well-groomed man is a huge turn-on.

Tip #7:

Find a good tailor; this applies to women as well. Fit is more important than fashion. Pants that are too long and that require hemming only make you look sloppy and shorter. With jackets, make sure fit is based on how they look on the shoulders. If the jacket is too big and boxy in that area, you will look heavier and less fit. When it comes to shirts, tucked in with a belt is usually best, unless you have a large belly. If that's the case, or you prefer your shirts untucked, have them tailored shorter so they don't look too long. You can also purchase from UNTUCKit. Sleeve length is also important, especially if you're shorter or have shorter arms. Rolling up your sleeves is one great way to hide excess length, but ideally, removing the excess fabric will make you look more proportioned, muscular, and fit.

Tip #8:

Invest in a stylish pair of glasses and sunglasses. This is important because, as an accessory you wear on your face, it's the first thing we'll pay attention to. Glasses can really make a fashion statement and can easily detract from or enhance your overall image. Ask someone you trust for help or find an experienced salesperson to help find the best styles that complement your facial features and head shape. As you get older, invest in a pair of dark-framed glasses. As Tom Ford so eloquently puts it, "Everything else can droop and slide, but that pair of dark glasses stays sharp and crisp."

Tip #9:

Hygiene is key. Halitosis is not your friend. Floss and keep mints or mouth spray in your car and coat pockets. Nothing kills a mood more than bad breath.

Tip #10:

Find your signature scent (this applies to ladies too!). Ask a salesperson or a friend to help you, if you're not sure what works for you. Remember that you should only be able to smell your cologne or perfume if you are within proximity—think "kissing distance." If I can smell you coming, it's too strong and a turn-off. Plus, for many people, it can cause a migraine or upset their allergies.

Tip #11:

While this has nothing to do with clothes, this is still a reflection of yourself: a sloppy, dirty car is a turn-off. Keep it clean, guys!

The idea of "fashion foreplay" is using what's available to sartorially shift your mindset into something sexier. It reflects how we feel inside. I never did make it to the sales floor at Victoria's Secret, but reflecting on what at first seemed to be a rather inconsequential time in my life of selling body butters, perfumes, and lotions turned out to be so important, as it showed me once again the power of clothing. I'll be discussing everything you need to know about the right undergarments for all body shapes in the "What's Underneath Matters Too" tutorial.

CHAPTER 12

A Foreign Exchange

"Remember that not getting what you want
is sometimes a wonderful stroke of luck."

—Dalai Lama

Let me begin by saying that this is one of the hardest chapters for me to write because it reveals sides of my past self that I'm quite ashamed of. In pursuit of attempting to fill the deep hole inside me, I lost perspective and I'm embarrassed of my own selfish needs and behavior.

It's the ugly parts that stemmed from my childhood wounds. In fact, when I finished writing the book, my son Jeremy read this chapter and said, "Mom, you can't write this. It makes you sound so shallow."

He's right, and while he's being protective of his mother and how readers might perceive me, it *is* a part of my story. The truth is, I *was* shallow. I was a young mom, overwhelmed, and still unhealed.

In my own need to fill a void, which was solely based on my adolescent desires of what I thought constituted a mother-daughter bond, my motives were self-centered. But it's an important story because it's one that taught me the greatest lessons and healed me in the process.

I have learned that what screws me up the most in life is the picture in my head of how things are *supposed* to be. When I learn to love without conditions and let go of the outcome, along with my expectations, I grow and find inner peace.

When I was pregnant with my first child, I knew, without a shadow of a doubt, that I was going to have a son. After all, that's all I knew, having grown up surrounded by males. And when I found out I was pregnant with my second child, as much as I had hoped for a girl, I once again had a visceral knowing that I would be blessed with another son. So, when my husband came home one day from work, after having just attended a rotary meeting and suggested that we house a female foreign exchange student, I was intrigued by the idea. At first, I was slightly apprehensive; my kids were very young and in elementary school. But the more I thought about the prospect of having some female energy in the house, the more excited I became.

He handed me some paperwork for a sixteen-year-old high schooler who lived in Beijing. She was an only child, spoke English, was a straight-A student, was in choir, and played on the basketball team in school. She seemed perfect on paper, and I became preoccupied with the fantasy that I would finally have someone to share all my girliness with, filling the void of not having the mother-daughter bond I had always wanted. So, once I agreed that we would be the "parents" of Zhi Ruo for her first semester in high school, I enrolled her at the local high school and my husband pulled some strings to get her into the school choir and onto the basketball team.

The closer we came to welcoming Zhi Ruo into our home, the more I fantasized about things I thought mothers and daughters do together. I was going to teach her everything I knew about fashion, makeup, and cooking. I envisioned us watching girly movies that my sons refused to watch and go for mani-pedis. We would talk about books and discuss important subject matter, like how to be empowered as women and how to be brave and limitless in our lives. We would chat about boys, and I could give her advice on my experience, having been surrounded predominantly by males. I could picture us enjoying high tea, scones, and chocolates. And, of course, we would go shopping together and I would share with her my love of clothes. I was clueless, and I thought that these were the types of things that were important in creating a mother-daughter bond because I had never experienced it firsthand. I had this romantic notion that I would finally be able to fill that hole that was missing in my heart.

Zhi arrived on her sixteenth birthday. All the foreign exchange students were brought to one central home, a thirty-minute drive from where we lived. Before heading out to pick her up, I decorated the house with pink and silver balloons for her birthday and a WELCOME banner sprawled across the stair banister in the foyer. I had asked my husband to pick up a birthday cake, chocolate, of course, because that's my favorite, and I was hoping hers too. When I arrived at the central home, I parked my car and sat there for a moment as I watched excited boys and girls load their luggage into their new host families' cars. I was so excited too, and I had a picture in my mind of what I thought Zhi would look like in person. Which was based on a gender stereotype that stemmed from my immaturity and further embedded from religious upbringing. For the last several weeks, I had been envisioning all the things I had always wanted to do if I had a mother when I was a teenager.

Since I am the epitome of a girly girl, I assumed that Zhi would be too. So, when I saw her waiting timidly in the corner of the room, I was quite surprised at her appearance. She had a short razor-style haircut with heavy, thick long bangs that hung into her eyes, which, in my opinion, detracted from her beautiful round face. She wore sneakers, a pair of oversize, long board shorts, and a button-down flannel, concealing her body. She was what one might refer to back in the day (and politically incorrect) as a "tomboy." I approached her and introduced myself. She did not make much eye contact with me and seemed, understandably, shy and frightened.

One of the things I noticed immediately was the way she walked. Her feet barely came off the ground, and her arms remained mostly motionless. She moved very slowly and methodically, vastly different from our fast-paced culture. She was graceful, yet her posture and poise lacked confidence. I could sense that she was insecure and uncomfortable in her own skin, as most sixteen-year-olds are. From my stylistic point of view and my expertise as an image consultant and stylist, I personally thought her clothes and her hairstyle detracted from her natural beauty. She had a beautiful porcelain-like round face, and her hairstyle didn't complement its structure. I especially loved when she smiled because her eyes would sparkle, and you could see her big dimples.

Once we were in the car, I turned to her and wished her a happy birthday, which caught her by surprise. I later learned that her parents didn't celebrate her birthday, at least not in the way Western cultures do. After a few minutes of driving, I turned to her and asked if there was any particular food she didn't like. She stared at me for a moment with her big dark-brown eyes, like a deer in the headlights. She must have been so terrified. After all, she just left her parents and the only country she had ever known, flew on a plane for thirteen hours, and was now sitting next to complete strangers who would be her guardians for the next six months. Then she reached into her backpack and pulled out her digital translator and began typing. After a moment of silence, she looked up at me and said, "Chocolate." For a moment, I thought I didn't hear her correctly. *Did she just say chocolate? That can't be possible,* I thought. Anyone who knows me knows I have a special relationship with chocolate. I actually sometimes think I have another stomach for chocolate, because no matter how much food I consume at a meal, I will *never* turn down chocolate. *How could she have an aversion to my favorite comfort food?* Well, I guess she wouldn't be eating her birthday cake or enjoying chocolates at the Peninsula Hotel.

During the drive home, Zhi looked pale, as though she was going to be sick. She asked if she could roll the windows down and was quiet for the remainder of the drive. When we pulled up to the house, she looked like she was just about to doze off to sleep. We later learned that she didn't usually travel by car and mostly used the subway or her bicycle as modes of transportation. The motion made her carsick and, incidentally, also very sleepy. So, for the duration of her stay with us, it wasn't uncommon for Zhi to fall asleep along with my two young sons next to her.

In the beginning, it was difficult to communicate with Zhi and there were a lot of cultural differences I hadn't considered. We even had trouble properly pronouncing her name, which was hilarious. She was so polite that it took her several days to gently point out that we were butchering the pronunciation. She eventually came up with an American name to simplify our lives. She would give herself an all-American name: Kathy. It was also difficult to get her to adjust to our overscheduled American fast-paced lifestyle.

I was constantly rushing her to avoid being late. She also wasn't used to being alone. She lived in a high-rise in the crowded capital city of China, sharing a one-bedroom apartment with her parents. She had never slept alone before, and I suspect she was afraid to do so because she slept with a small stuffed animal and kept a night-light on during most of her stay. I could relate to being afraid of the dark. I was plagued with nightmares as a child and often crawled into bed with my older brother Philip, even throughout my teenage years. I enjoyed having Zhi around me because she had a sweet and gentle spirit about her. I liked her energy and enjoyed her company. But sometimes I felt like I had a shadow, and the things I hoped she might want to partake in, she had no interest in, like learning how to cook. So, I was now catering to three children and a husband, all with different palates. It was exhausting.

Several days after she arrived and we all started to feel more comfortable, we surprised her and told her we were able to get her on the basketball team. This was no easy feat, and the coach had to go to upper authority to get permission to allow her to be on the team without having gone through tryouts. Zhi was ecstatic and wanted to start practicing right away.

My husband Tony put up the basketball hoop, and they all planned to head outside after dinner to shoot some hoops. Zhi went upstairs to put on her basketball jersey and a pair of basketball shorts while the boys waited for her outside. I stayed in the kitchen to clean up after dinner and prepare bath time for the boys. I was still cleaning the kitchen when they returned from shooting hoops . Tony walked past me with a mysterious look on his face. Zhi retired to her room for the night, and I got the boys into bed as I anxiously waited to hear what Tony was going to tell me. Turns out, Zhi's "basketball skills" were less than stellar. Incidentally, we learned that she had never actually played basketball, but that she had always wanted to. This obviously posed a conundrum, as we had put a lot of effort into getting her on the team. I was concerned that she would be kicked off the team or, worse, made fun of. So, we decided that we would have a discussion with her and try to convince her to resign and solely focus on her singing talent.

In the morning, we explained to Zhi that she might not have the skills necessary to play basketball on the team and that the high school team is one of the top-ranking ones in California. This did not seem to deter her. She was determined and promised to practice every day until she got better. We reached out to the basketball coach and explained the situation, and he thankfully suggested that she remain on the team and practice with them but not actually play in the games. When we told her what the coach agreed to and asked her if she still wanted to remain on the team under these conditions, she was thrilled.

School was fast approaching, and I wanted to take Zhi shopping for school supplies and a new outfit to wear on her first day of school. When you grow up with an absent mother and an abusive alcoholic surrogate, there are certain times during your childhood that are more painful than others. For me, it wasn't the birthdays or the holidays but the small subtle moments in life that reminded me of my solitude and made the void in my heart ache a little more. The beginning of each school year was particularly difficult for me. Everyone seemed prepared but me. My surrogate was sleeping, angry, hungover, or nowhere to be found, so I was pretty much on my own to prepare for the new school year. I would ride the bus alone to the store for school supplies, where I would see parents, mostly mothers, with their children buying the necessary items needed for each class subject. I could never quite figure out what to purchase and always felt unprepared and embarrassed.

One year, I asked my friend Laura if I could join her and her mom when they went shopping. I don't know why this made me so sad, but as her mom continued gathering school supplies, I became acutely aware of the emptiness in my heart and started to feel like I was going to cry. It was during these simple yet utterly unpredictable moments that I couldn't suppress my emotions. The reality of living in a dysfunctional family without any parental guidance bubbled up inside me, and I felt like I couldn't hold back the tears any longer and excused myself and ran to the bathroom. I locked myself in the stall and allowed the floodgates to release until I heard the door open and someone came in. I wiped my face and returned as if nothing had happened. I was good like that. I could bury things deep down, and no one knew that I felt broken.

When we were finished at the drugstore, I went over to my friend's house to play. We went into her room to put away her new things and, sprawled out across her bed, were multiple outfits neatly organized with the tags still attached. She said they were options for the first day of school and she wanted my help deciding which outfit to choose. They were neatly organized with pants, shirts, accessories, socks, underwear, and even shoes. I thought this was a genius idea because I was always late and stressed out over what to wear. She was most excited about her new Guess jeans with the flaps that everyone was coveting at the time.

One by one, she unfolded each outfit to show me. Then there was a knock at the door, and her mom peeked inside and handed her a fanny pack. She thanked her mom and opened it up in front of me. It was neatly packed with tampons, sanitary pads, and deodorant. Once again, my heart sank, and I longed for a mother. I was jealous of it all. When I left her house to walk home, I'd made a vow right then and there: my children would always have all their school supplies, a new outfit for the first day of school, and a fanny pack with all the essentials (that is, of course, if I had girls). Perhaps I owe that childhood best friend some credit today because, in addition to keeping the promise I made when I was just twelve years old, a large part of my business is organizing my clients' wardrobes into digital lookbooks. I like to think that the idea came from the memory of watching her arrange all her clothes on her bed so long ago.

Anticipating her excitement, I asked Zhi if she wanted to go shopping to get school supplies and if I could buy her a new outfit for the first day of school. I was surprised by her lack of enthusiasm. She hesitated for a minute and then said, "I guess?"

I was confused by her aloof and disinterested response. After all, a shopping spree was a fantasy for me as a teenager entering high school.

"Are you okay? Is something bothering you?" I asked.

She said she wanted to get her school supplies, but she wasn't interested in shopping for clothes. I was confused, and this threw me for a loop because this wasn't what I had pictured in my head as our "mother-daughter" bonding time.

When I asked her why she didn't like shopping, she said it was because she didn't think she was pretty and was self-conscious about her body. I dug a little deeper, and she opened up to me about her relationship with her father. She told me that her father never told her that she was pretty and, on the contrary, alluded that she wasn't attractive, but that she was *smart*. Our fathers' value systems were diametrically opposed. My father put a lot of emphasis on my looks and never recognized my intellect, while Zhi's did exactly the opposite. I could really feel her pain. She also divulged that he had wanted a son, and she thought he was disappointed when she was born.

Then, in what I had thought was a moment of sudden insight, I reasoned that this was perhaps why the universe had brought us together. I was going to help her see her beauty and her femininity, and I would start by introducing her to wardrobe and fashion. I reassured her that she was beautiful and insisted that I would make the experience fun and would help her find clothes that would enhance her beauty and make her feel more confident. She reluctantly agreed.

We arrived at the mall, and I looked over at her; once again, she was struck with motion sickness and was fast asleep. I woke her up, and we headed into Nordstrom so I could help her discover and embrace a new image. As we passed the boys' department, Zhi stopped and said, "Can I look here?"

"This is the boys' department," I replied, confused.

"Yes, I know," she said. I noted that the girls' department was upstairs, but she insisted.

"I would like to look here, please," she replied.

Zhi proceeded to the boys' department and began looking through the racks, eventually pulling out an army of Anorak. She put it on and looked in the mirror and smiled.

"I like it. This okay?" she asked.

"Um, I guess, but don't you want to look upstairs in the girls' department too?" I pushed.

"No, I like this," she replied.

"Okay, if this makes you feel good and happy, then let's get it." I paid for the jacket, and she thanked me and asked if we could go home now. I urged her to go upstairs, perhaps scour some cute dresses that she could wear underneath her new jacket. She very politely refused, and then she asked if she could look for army boots.

As we walked through the mall toward the shoe store, I continued to make my futile attempts at awakening her girliness, pointing out feminine summer dresses, floral tops, and sandals, but she remained uninterested. Indeed, it didn't seem as though she was enjoying the shopping process, despite my best efforts.

Other than the army jacket, Zhi didn't try on anything else that day. We left the mall with the jacket and a pair of Doc Martens. I was speechless. I must confess I was also slightly disappointed that we would not be spending our time on the weekends shopping together. Once again, my preconceived idea of our "mother-daughter" bonding over shopping and fashion was not meeting my expectations, but I really had no one else to blame other than myself. I was dead set on my idea of bonding with my "daughter" without even opening up to the possibility that she might not want that or be interested.

Later that evening, I knocked on her door and handed her a makeup bag with some feminine hygiene products for her backpack. After all, it was the thing I had always wanted from a mother figure.

Zhi started school, and life got complicated. Three different schools and three different pickups and drop-offs. Sports practices, choir rehearsals, little league, homework, birthday parties, and playdates. Our lives changed drastically once school started and, I'm ashamed to admit this, but I started feeling resentful and overwhelmed. In addition to feeling like a taxi driver, our family trips didn't feel like real vacations anymore because now I was taking care of three children. Zhi must have felt lonely and was also vying for our attention. I thought it was because she was an only child and was not used to sharing the limelight. It was difficult balancing the needs of my own children with our now "third child," someone who had entered our life from a culture so different from our own.

One weekend, Zhi had an event in Huntington Beach about an hour and a half from my house. Just before leaving to pick her up, I received a phone call from another host family who lived thirty minutes north of us.

They were in a bind and needed a favor and asked if I could pick up their foreign exchange student when I picked up Zhi and bring her to our home. So, I drove to Huntington Beach to pick up Zhi and Sophia. Sophia had long brown hair, golden skin, and big beautiful brown eyes. She was wearing a white eyelet fit-and-flare dress, a denim jacket with silver embellished metallic sandals, and lip gloss. Her demeanor was cheerful and spirited.

Shortly after we got into the car and Zhi dozed off to sleep, I asked Sophia how she was liking California.

"I love it here," she replied with a heavy Italian accent.

"And how do you like your host family?" I inquired. She hesitated for a moment and then said she didn't like them that much; they were "boring" in her words. Ouch.

I was surprised. "What makes them boring?"

"We don't go anywhere. I love the cinema, and food, and I love to cook and to shop. The missus, she doesn't like to do anything like that," she said.

My heart sank into my stomach. I couldn't believe my ears. She likes to cook and shop? I'm embarrassed to admit, but my first thought was that Sophia might have been a better fit for me.

Sophia and I talked the entire ride home, and the more we talked, the more disappointed I became that Zhi's interests were vastly different than mine, and all the things I previously fantasized about doing with Zhi never happened. I began to descend into self-pity. This experience was not at all what I had envisioned it would be. Zhi was polite and kind, but at times her stay with us felt mostly like work with not much reward. When Zhi moved to her next host family her second semester in high school, we were sad to see her go, but also relieved. The truth is, we weren't a match for her either. Zhi needed someone who wasn't always on the go and who didn't have small children. A family that could give her the love and attention she deserved. We said goodbye to her, and that was that.

As the years passed, I would reflect on our experience together but was never able to grasp the bigger meaning of why the universe had brought the two of us together. What was the lesson I needed to learn? I also wondered why Zhi had never reached out to us after she left; perhaps she felt culturally isolated. I assumed it was because she was selfish; looking back, I should have considered my own role and my own selfishness.

Then one early Saturday morning ten years later, my phone rang. "Hello, Jen?" I heard a familiar voice on the other end.

"Yes?"

"Hi, it's Zhi!"

"Zhi?" It took me a minute to place her voice. I was shocked to hear from her. "How are you? I'm so surprised to hear from you."

"I'm here. I'm back in the States. Could you come pick me up? I want to see you and the boys."

She asked if we could pick her up the next day in Camarillo, about twenty minutes away from our home. At first, that old, frustrated feeling came back to being the family taxi driver. But it also had been ten years since our last visit, and I was thrilled to see her. "Sure, you could come for an early dinner. I'll pick you up at four," I replied, somewhat reluctantly.

That night, I pulled out some old pictures of when Zhi was living with us to remind the kids of what she looked like and the adventures and activities that we did together. After all, they were just six and eight years of age the last time they saw her.

I picked up the first picture and smiled at her beautiful face with her big, adorable dimples. One by one, I looked at the pictures and a strange feeling poured over me. I started remembering these tender moments when she and my boys would play the guitar and sing together for hours, or when we all rocked out in the car to a famous Chinese rap artist she was obsessed with. Her childlike excitement over seeing rabbits and deer for the first time roaming in the open fields that surrounded our home. Or how she would sit in the dugout regardless of the dreadful summer heat, cheering the boys on when they were up at bat. I started getting flooded with memories that at the time I didn't give much heed to before.

Suddenly time shifted and slowed. It felt like I was watching an old movie being played back in slow motion. I could see Zhi beaming, with her huge dimples, at her choir performances as she sang proudly to us. How fearless she was in the vast Pacific Ocean as she bodysurfed with my boys for hours. How she never was embarrassed to try new things, even if she wasn't good at them.

I remembered the enormous stuffed animal she refused to put down at Disneyland, which she carried all day and night; Tony had won it for her by shooting baskets into the hoop. How proud she was each and every time she introduced us to someone she knew and how she would say, "This is my American family." The family vacations we took in our motor home, where we sat outside around a campfire and made s'mores. The way she would proudly show me her cleanly shaven legs and laugh, and the candid talks we had about her parents and how she wished she could live in the States.

How, every once in a while, she would come downstairs wearing something completely out of her comfort zone and spin around and ask my opinion. How appreciative she was to have her first Easter basket, which my mother-in-law gave her, and her childlike excitement as she looked for hidden Easter eggs. The respect she had for our Jewish traditions and her love of smoked salmon and potato latkes. It's interesting how humans are wired. How we tend to naturally have a negative bias because it takes up more of an emotional charge. Before Zhi had called that day, my memories of our experiences were adverse ones and mostly centered on my expectations.

Suddenly my heart softened, as if I were given a new set of lenses and stepped outside my own consciousness. As I sat there remembering these things, it dawned on me that she wasn't competing with my boys for attention; she needed attention. I realized how much I admired her thirst for adventure and knowledge of the world.

That night sitting on my floor, with all these pictures spread out on the carpet, I tried to imagine what it would have been like for Zhi to leave her family for the first time and travel across the world all alone, to another culture with a different language at the age of sixteen. It must have been so frightening for her, yet she persevered. I thought about her determination to stay on the basketball team despite her ability, her courage to take risks to acclimate to her new environment. I thought about how brave she was to leave the only home she ever knew and embrace each and every opportunity that was presented to her; her thirst for adventure and knowledge of the world and her willingness to try anything despite fear.

Zhi never complained, and although not very helpful around the house, it was my lack of understanding her culture and my unrealistic expectations that was the crux of my disappointment. I had never taken the time to look through Zhi's eyes. I was so preoccupied with the silly romantic notion of what I thought would bond us, like shopping and cooking, because those were some of the things I missed as a teenager. I was so focused on all the things she wasn't that I was missing all the little things she *was*. I felt ashamed at that moment; I was embarrassed of myself.

That next day, I prepared some of Zhi's favorite foods, like potato latkes and noodle kugel, and picked up a non-chocolate dessert and headed to Camarillo to pick her up from the same house I had picked her up from exactly ten years earlier. When I arrived, I called her cell phone and waited in the driveway for her to come out. Suddenly a grown woman appeared gracefully, walking toward the car. Her long, silky shiny hair hung just above her waist (much more flattering on her beautiful face), and she was wearing a colorful fit-and-flare dress, dainty jewelry, a cardigan sweater, and small kitten heels. My jaw dropped; I couldn't believe my eyes. Zhi, now twenty-six years old, had stepped into her true self and broken away from her father's judgment. She was always beautiful, but now she had a confidence about her that was unmistakable. We talked the entire ride home, and she told me about all her adventures since leaving our home.

Tony and the boys were just as excited to see her as I was, and although the boys hadn't seen her in ten years, Zhi had a way about her that just made you feel like nothing had changed. She wasn't embarrassed to try anything, and she could just jump right back in as if no time had passed. She grabbed the guitar and started playing and singing; it all felt familiar, nostalgic, and even familial. During dinner, we reminisced about all the things we had done together, and she filled us in on her life since leaving the Principe home. She went back to China to finish high school and then applied to the University of California, where she was accepted and had since graduated from. She told us about her serious American boyfriend, how she lived alone, secured a full-time job in the United States, and was financially independent.

I was so proud of her and admired her determination to create a life for herself. She had come a long way from sleeping with a stuffed animal and a night-light. And I thought to myself, if I had a daughter, I would want her to be just like Zhi.

We asked her why she didn't keep in touch with us. She responded by saying that she didn't want to inconvenience or bother us because she knew how busy we were. Once again, I felt ashamed that we were always rushed and didn't have more patience with her, and that my first thought was that *she* was being selfish. On the contrary, she was being thoughtful.

Then Tony asked her a simple question that changed my entire perspective about why she came into our lives. He asked her, "What was the most influential thing that happened while you were in the United States?" She paused for a moment, and then she looked right at me, in my eyes, and said, "Jen."

I was shocked. *How?* I thought.

She said that when she arrived, she felt insecure and unattractive. I had always told her that she was beautiful, but initially she didn't believe me, even when I persisted in reminding her.

"It didn't matter what I wore. Jen always said I was pretty and smart," Zhi continued.

She went on to say I made her feel comfortable in trying new fashion styles and to embrace having fun with clothes. She said she had studied me and watched the way I dressed myself, how I took pride in my appearance, and how I easily embraced my femininity. She said she wanted that too but was afraid she wouldn't be accepted.

By the time she left, she had made a promise to herself that when she returned to China, she would stop worrying about what her father thought, or her friends, and start dressing in a way that fully expressed who she was; the person she *wanted* to be. That doesn't surprise me at all; Zhi had always been courageous and determined. When she made up her mind to do something, there would be no stopping her.

Sometimes, we just don't know the influence we have on others or the lessons we are meant to learn about the people who come into our lives (and why) until we are ready. Things take time to cultivate, and seeds were being planted in both of us.

That night brought a lot of closure and clarity about why Zhi and I were brought together in this lifetime. Perhaps my role was simply to help Zhi see her beauty and femininity and embrace the fun in fashion. But Zhi's role in my life turned out to be much more profound. I learned that dressing to embrace your femininity doesn't necessarily mean the same thing for everyone. Zhi was feminine and beautiful regardless of what she wore. Sex and gender aren't perfectly binary, and neither is fashion. Ultimately, you should embrace clothes that simultaneously allow you to feel confident and comfortable in your own skin, regardless of how those clothes are "gendered."

I also learned that I missed a greater opportunity to have formed a deeper relationship with Zhi because of my own expectations. I was so busy looking at what I was getting out of the relationship rather than what I could *give* to it. Zhi taught me about taking the time to learn about cultural differences and that some things are not always as they appear. Sophia, the Italian foreign exchange student, might have shopped and cooked and fit perfectly into what I conceived of in a mother-daughter fantasy, but my healing would have only been temporary. I had to accept that I couldn't create a mother-daughter bond that doesn't exist and that my healing isn't a hole to be filled but a truth to be accepted.

After we finished dinner, we looked through old photos and reminisced about all the fun times we shared. Zhi reminded us of some of the funnier moments during her stay, like when she wanted to go out on her first date and I scared him off by asking him too many personal questions; or when the refrigerator broke in the motor home and our trip began with the lingering smell of rotten fish sticks. Later that night, we all drove her back to Camarillo to drop her off at that same house I picked her up at exactly a decade earlier. It felt different this time; it was harder to say goodbye. We had all changed, both physically and mentally. I knew deep down that our karmic contract was fulfilled and that this time I was really going to miss her.

When I think about Zhi, I'm thankful that our meeting was so fortuitous and that I was able, in some small way, to have had an impact on her life. Being a woman isn't about wearing kitten heels and having long hair. It's about being who you want to be and stepping into yourself. I was proud of her and that she had found her voice and stopped suppressing who she was to please others. Her appearance that day was a symbolic visual representation of her individuating from her father. More importantly, I'm grateful for the profound reflection she offered me, even if it came a decade after our initial meeting. Zhi possesses all the qualities I would want if I had had a daughter of my own, and her parents should be very proud of her. As her "American mom," I know I am.

CHAPTER 13

If It Sounds Too Good to Be True, It Probably Is

"True humility is not thinking less of yourself; it's thinking of yourself less."

— C. S. Lewis

This chapter could be its own book or, quite frankly, a movie. This is a story about trying to force pieces that don't fit, not listening to your inner voice, and getting back up when you've been knocked down hard! It's about that old adage: "If it sounds too good to be true, it probably is," and when it rang true for me.

In the beginning of my styling career, I was referred to Karen by my very close friend Samantha. Karen was beautiful—a hard-working businesswoman, married to a successful plastic surgeon. She was someone who wore her heart on her sleeve, and during my first visit with her, she broke down in tears as she opened up to me about her low self-esteem, anxiety, and depression. It's not unusual for a client to become vulnerable while inside the closet, as it's such an intimate and private space. She also revealed to me that her twins had disabilities and that she hadn't had any time to invest in her appearance. My heart broke for her, and I really wanted to help her feel better about herself. It's a scenario I've seen play out so many times throughout my styling career since, and I was excited to improve her life through the joy of clothing.

Within a short period, I could begin to see her transformation and her self-esteem soar. We ditched the outdated, bejeweled True Religion jeans and crop tops, plunging necklines, and tacky minidresses to a more updated, refined, tasteful, and sexier version. She was excited about going on dates with her husband again and being more social with her friends and community. She was so energized and excited about her new style and image that, to me, seemed like she was on a high.

Karen was a loving wife and doted over her husband, Brad. She wanted him to have the same experience that she had since working together with me and asked me to style him too. So, I revamped his wardrobe as well. I traded in his boring polos for some patterned, well-fitted shirts and updated his oversize, outdated suits to a more modern GQ look, and the two of them looked and felt great. They both were very kind and appreciative and always paid me in a timely fashion.

Over time, I could sense that Karen wanted to have a friendship with me outside of our business relationship. She started inviting me over to her family barbecues and would rave to her family and friends about how wonderful I was and how she considered me family. And that was the first warning bell that I ignored. In my book, friends don't become family unless they have earned that place, which takes trust and time to cultivate.

But Karen was one of those people who truly wanted success for those she loved and believed had talent. I happened to be one of those people. She was very supportive of my styling career and used to say that I was a hidden gem, that she wanted the world to discover me. At that time, I was only three years into my styling career, and I must admit I wanted that too. She was constantly coming up with ideas on how to grow my business and collaborate. One of the ideas she had been working on in her husband's practice was to offer a wellness program dedicated to providing body, mind, and soul healing to their post-op patients. Within this service, I would curate a new wardrobe as part of their weight loss experience, since much of his practice revolved around weight loss surgery. And this concierge-type service could be built into the surgery fee. Brilliant!

As Karen continued developing her wellness program, I continued styling her for her different business engagements and social events. She was always gracious and thankful. But the longer we worked together, the more I noticed her unpredictable moods. Some days, she was on a high, overly excited with her newest ideas and full of compliments, while on others, she was moody, irritable, and snappy. Occasionally, when I showed up for our scheduled appointment, she looked like she hadn't slept in days. I assumed it was because she was parenting her two special needs children. I was worried about her, and sometimes I would call Samantha to express my concern. Samantha felt something wasn't right too, but she could never really put her finger on what it was.

One day, I got a call from Karen out of the blue. "Hi, Jen?" Her voice sounded excited on the other end of the phone.

"Oh, hi, Karen, how are you?" I replied.

"I'm fantastic, Jen. Are you sitting down?"

"Yes, is everything okay?" I asked.

"Better than okay. Remember how I said I believed in you, and how I wanted the world to know you? Well, I'm going to make that happen."

I was confused. "What do you mean?"

"Well, I have an opportunity for all of us. I have been contacted by the US Doctors of Africa and the United Nations Office for Partnerships. They are in strategic collaboration with a member organization of thirty-five African First Ladies who will be attending a Health Summit Round Table here in Los Angeles. Basically, Jen, they are here to raise funds and awareness on health, education, and the eradication of poverty in Africa. Are you still with me?" she asked.

"Yes, I'm listening," I said, wondering what this all had to do with me.

"After the weeklong summit, there's a sponsorship opportunity to provide the First Ladies of Africa and their entourage a day to enjoy a wellness getaway. Brad and I have decided to be a sponsor and host the wellness day. Jen, this is the perfect opportunity to introduce the First Ladies to the mind, body, and spirit surgical experience. I'm proposing that we host a luncheon with a fashion show along with pop-up shops of all the highest end retail stores in Los Angeles and Beverly Hills," she continued. "Here's where you come in: I want you to curate the most impressive fashion event we have ever seen in this community and handle all the retail pop-up shops. I want runway models, gorgeous high-end clothes, and the works. I want it to be over the top, and I want to blow everyone away. Are you interested?"

I began to feel overwhelmed and, still, slightly confused. I thanked her for thinking of me, and she started rambling again. It sounded like she was on a high, like the Energizer Bunny. I could feel her excitement and enthusiasm on the other end of the phone.

"Here's the best part: last year these ladies spent upward of one million dollars each on retail therapy. You will be their private liaison to the fashion world. They will set up private shopping appointments with you during their stay because it's critical that they keep their retail spending out of the public eye. After all, they are here raising funds for Africa," she said.

It was a lot to take in, but I began feeding off her excitement. I was new in my career and wanted to be discovered. I could see how this could really advance my career, while at the same time, be a part of such an important cause.

"Are you interested?" she asked again.

"Hell yes, I'm interested!" I said. "Is there a budget for the fashion show and for my services?"

"Yes, one hundred fifty thousand dollars that was donated by the consulate general for the US Doctors of Africa. So, tell me what you would charge for an event like this and send me a proposal. It is a charity event, Jen, so please keep that in mind."

"Yes, of course. When is it?"

"Well, that's the only caveat. It's in three weeks. But I know that you can pull this together. I believe in you," she reiterated.

Red flag number two. These kinds of events typically take months of planning in advance. My head was swirling. There were a few things that didn't make sense to me, like, Why would the consulate general give her $150,000 to host an event? Why not just donate the money to the charity? But I was green and eager, so I ignored the signs.

Karen said she would be hosting a dinner the next night to discuss details and to meet the US Doctors of Africa and the chief of the UNOP.

"I have also asked Samantha and her husband Scott [also a doctor] to join us. I think this would be a great opportunity to get them involved too. Why don't you and Tony join us? We can iron out all the details," she offered.

I agreed, she repeated her excitement, and we hung up.

The next evening, Tony and I made our way to one of the most prestigious golf country clubs in the world, where the dinner was hosted. It was also where the proposed luncheon and fashion show were to be held. When we arrived, we were escorted into a private dining room, where eight guests were already seated.

Karen and Brad stood up to greet and introduce us. "This is Tony and Jennifer Principe. They are leaders in this community and will be a wonderful addition to the annual summit. Oh, and by the way, Jen is an incredible stylist, and she is in charge of the fashion event and the retail therapy aspect of the wellness day."

Then one by one, she went around the room and introduced us: Samantha and Scott (my friends); Karen and Diana, the marketing team behind the first summit; Carl, the head of US Doctors of Africa; and a man named George, a UN representative.

All seemed legitimate so far. We shook hands and exchanged niceties. Tony and I made our way to the two empty seats next to Carl and George. Just as I was about to sit in my chair, Karen asked if she could speak to me privately for a moment. I walked out of the room with her. "Jen, please don't discuss the budget for the event or your fees with Carl or George—or with anyone, for that matter. Carl has asked to remain anonymous with his donation, and I would like to honor his request," she said, in a hushed tone.

"Absolutely," I assured her. I really didn't think much about her request until later.

Back at dinner, I thought to myself how much of an honor it was to be asked to style the event. When Carl turned to me and graciously thanked me for my generosity, I told him that I should be thanking *him* for helping make this happen.

Then Karen stood up to speak. "I want to welcome all of you and thank you for being a part of this impactful cultural, social, and philanthropic event that we will be hosting at this prestigious location. Each of you is integral to the success of the event, and we couldn't do this without you. So, thank you from the bottom of our hearts. We will be hosting the wellness luncheon and fashion show and anticipate two hundred fifty very influential guests to attend. There are several sponsorship opportunities left for individuals and corporations to host a table and create a relationship with these First Ladies. I will be sending each of you a welcome and information package to send to your friends and business associates. This is an exclusive, once-in-a-lifetime opportunity, and sponsorship is limited."

Then she went on about public and private investors, stakeholders, healthcare infrastructure, etc. Everything sounded legitimate, and I was really excited to be a part of such an important cause and event. This was an incredible opportunity, but I knew I had a lot of work ahead of me in the next three weeks.

When I got home that night, there was an email from Karen sitting in my inbox, which I had missed prior to our dinner. The subject line: TIME TO SHINE! YOUR RESPONSIBILITIES. In addition to the fashion event, and the pop-up retail stores, Karen asked that I provide impressive gift bags for each of the First Ladies upon their arrivals. She wanted a stylist presentation package immediately listing my fees and services offered so that they could begin scheduling private shopping appointments with me. Finally, she would be attending all the weeklong summit meetings that other companies were hosting and needed me to style her and Brad for each of the events, free of charge.

It was overwhelming, to say the least, but I didn't lose track that it was, ultimately, for a good cause. I emailed my fee structure over to Karen that evening and decided to donate half of my fee back to the organization. I also agreed to style them for each of the upcoming summit events at no cost. I was very grateful for the opportunity, and that was my way of thanking her. Karen replied immediately, thanking me for my generosity. The following day, I received this email:

> *Dear friends:*
>
> *I just want to be sure that you all understand the invitation process designed to protect the diplomats attending the upcoming events. Our purpose is to allow only a limited number of VIP guests access to these events so that we may ensure an*

intimate, relaxed environment for all. No photography will be allowed, unless it is preauthorized through my office.

There are several opportunities for individuals and corporations to host unique events and to create a relationship with the First Ladies. Those who sponsor will be afforded the opportunity to contribute their specialty and receive media coverage.

Due to strict security limitations, this event is considered exclusive. Only invitees who reference a sponsor's name will be entitled to purchase tickets for this event. Because space is extremely limited and the timing for the event is quickly approaching, we encourage you to forward the attached invitation to any members of your inner circle that would like to attend the rare opportunity to interact face-to-face with these powerful decision makers.

Many thanks to my wonderful friends, who recognized this opportunity to give back and make a significant difference in the world.

In love we trust,

Karen

In hindsight, the letter had inconsistencies all throughout. On the one hand, she was asking us to help find sponsors, yet the letter made it seem like the event was *very* exclusive and space was limited. I didn't pay too much attention to it, though, because I was focused on the fashion event and how I was going to pull *that* off in three weeks. Sam and Karen went to a high-end invitation company to design the invitations, which were supposed to be sent out immediately.

Samantha called me after their meeting, concerned that Karen was being too extravagant. She said the invitations Karen had picked were *over-the-top* exorbitant and ridiculously expensive. When she questioned Karen about the unnecessary expense, Karen reassured her about her very large budget and that the invitations needed to reflect the caliber of the event. Karen also began expanding the wellness event to include an overnight at a local five-star hotel, with breakfast and more roundtable discussions. It began feeling like a grandiose plan to keep these First Ladies captive as long as she could. Samantha and I began having some uneasy feelings, but we both ignored them.

I canceled all my clients for the next three weeks and hired two full-time employees. I began working with my computer graphic designer to create pamphlets with my logo and fee structure to get to Karen as quickly as possible so I could begin setting up styling appointments. In addition, I created some marketing materials to present to my retail stores about the upcoming event. My out-of-pocket expenses were beginning to add up.

My first appointment was with the head of Neiman Marcus in Beverly Hills, but they quickly declined the "opportunity" and said that these events are planned a year in advance, and it would not be feasible for them to be involved. I did everything to convince them, but they knew something I didn't (*yet*): that these things take *time* to plan. Disappointed but determined, my next appointment was with Barneys. Again, they declined, stating that they, too, couldn't get approval from corporate in such a short period of time. One by one, each large department store declined. I had spent a week already trying to get department store retailers involved, and I was beginning to worry that the time frame was too soon for me to pull this together.

That following week, my next appointments were with some of the most high-end boutiques in Beverly Hills, Pacific Palisades, Newport Beach, and Los Angeles. To my relief, one by one, each boutique agreed to loan me clothes, shoes, bags, and jewelry for the fashion event and set up a pop-up shop for the boutique. I was relieved but also stressed, as the event was quickly approaching; I still had so much to do.

Karen called and asked me to meet the party planner at the venue to discuss the fashion show layout and create the space for the pop-up shops. Karen was at the meeting, and as we were designing the room for the fashion show, she said that she was expecting even more guests than she originally planned; apparently tickets were being sold quickly and there was no room for a runway. With the additional tables needed for the luncheon, we just didn't have enough space.

I suddenly had a vision that the models would then be scattered around the perimeter of the room, each posed like an art painting inside large picture frames. Each picture frame would have a light at the top, and when it was a model's turn to walk the room, the light would go on in the picture frame signaling the audience where to look. The model would walk the room, adorned in the most fashionable clothing, and then return to the picture frame and strike a final pose. This would all be choreographed to music and solve the problem of the lack of space. Karen and the party planner loved the idea. But the picture frames needed to be built in time and could be expensive. Karen insisted that the cost was not an issue and that I must have these frames.

The next day, we received a call from the party planner with the estimate to build the frames in time: $5,000. Karen agreed to pay for the frames, saying they were "*a must.*" Meanwhile, I set appointments with all the boutiques to come to the country club to lay out the space needed for the pop-up shops, started collecting items for the gift bags, developed the fashion storyboard, sent over all my marketing materials, hired ten models for the fashion show, and was working with the DJ to synchronize the music for the framed catwalk—this, all while styling Karen and Brad for the various upcoming summit events they were going to be attending the following week. I also reached out to Rolls-Royce and Bentley of Beverly Hills and arranged to have the First Ladies picked up and brought to the country club the day of the event. With everything going on, it didn't occur to me that I hadn't received my check from Karen that we had agreed upon for the fashion event.

I was running all over town collecting gift bag items and pulling favors from all the stores I had created relationships with over the last three years. Barneys gave me a gift card for each First Lady, Gearys of Beverly Hills gave me a crystal bowl, Van Cleef & Arpels gave a keychain, various boutiques gave candles, and Damone Roberts ("The Eyebrow King") gave gift certificates for each lady.

Things were coming together, and all my stores were very excited to be a part of the event. On my way home, Karen called to remind me to send an email to my family and friends to purchase tickets because space was becoming limited. She said Shearson Lehman bought two tables and that various celebrities, including Angelina Jolie, would be attending. She also said the press contacted her and expected media coverage.

I was excited, nervous, and very confused at the same time. *Isn't this an exclusive event?* I thought that these First Ladies needed to be private about their retail shopping, so why would the media be there? But I didn't listen to the voice in my head, and I didn't ask any questions. I wanted to believe all the pieces would come together in the end; this would be my big break.

The week of the summit, Karen sent me her itinerary. She had a full schedule with summit roundtable meetings sponsored by other participants, elaborate dinners, and a backstage experience on the show *Dancing with the Stars*, all of which the First Ladies would be attending. While I was organizing looks for the models, I was shopping for Karen and Brad too. I was exhausted but determined to put my best foot forward and create a memorable event.

Up until this point, I still hadn't received a phone call to privately style any of the First Ladies, which was confusing. Then, seemingly out of the blue, I received a message from Karen on the first night of the summit. Our event was just five days away.

> Hi, honey, it's me. Thank you for styling me. I'm at the first event, and I feel amazing. Great job, once again. Listen, I'm locked up here with these First Ladies, and the party planner needs the deposit for the frames. She must have the money today, or the frames won't be done in time. Can you please meet her and write her a check for $5,000? I promise you, on my children's lives, I will pay you back *every* penny. This is going to be so amazing. Thanks, sweetheart. Oh, one more thing: I got you a ticket to the gala. It's the

night before our big event. You will be sitting at our table, and I will introduce you to these lovely ladies. They will probably book their styling appointments with you there, so bring your calendar. Thanks again.

Another warning bell went off in my head, but I felt conflicted. I had worked with Karen for a long time, and she *always* paid me before. The event was also around the corner, and the frames were an integral part of the show; without them, I'd have to rework the entire thing. All my boutiques had already set aside merchandise for the pop-up boutiques, and even the jewelry stores had ordered additional cases for their displays and had taken out insurance for the event. Time was ticking, and I was preoccupied with the scope of my job, but I failed, once again, to ask questions. I wrote the check and pressed on.

I did leave Karen a message asking when I would be hearing from the First Ladies about booking appointments. She replied via text, saying I should be getting calls soon.

I had ten models lined up for the fashion event, including a prior Mrs. Africa. Since I wasn't able to coordinate each model to be at the fittings, I hired two additional models to spend the next few days with me as I pulled together looks from various boutiques. We spent two full days creating looks and pulling merchandise. Once again, this was coming out of my pocket, and it was starting to add up.

Two days before the event, I loaned Karen a few dresses and some of my own personal jewelry for the *Dancing with the Stars* event and for the gala. I was running out of time to do private shopping for her, and she was on a tight budget from all the spending she was doing on the event. When I showed up at her house that morning, she looked like she had been up all night, with makeup from the night before still on her face. In her living room, there were papers scattered everywhere, and I noticed all the expensive boxed invitations still sitting across the floor that she picked out with Samantha. I was shocked to see she hadn't mailed them out.

Karen's behavior was frenetic; she wasn't making any sense to me. I asked her about the invitations, and she said don't worry about that, that she had everything under control. But I left her home with a pit in my stomach; something was definitely wrong.

I called Samantha, and she was concerned too. She said she noticed a lot of inconsistencies and that the last few times she spoke to Karen, she wasn't making any sense. I told Samantha about the invitations I found at her house, which was concerning to her too. That night, she was accompanying Karen to *Dancing with the Stars* and was going to get to the bottom of everything and report back to me. I was on pins and needles waiting to hear from her. I then got a text from her, reading, "She is acting strange, but all looks legitimate," with a photo attached of them backstage with one of the celebrity dancers. I breathed a sigh of relief.

The next morning, I headed back to the city to pull the rest of the clothes for the fashion show. I had my assistants at my home steaming and categorizing the clothes and taping the shoes. I had been working from the crack of dawn until midnight the last few nights finalizing all the details and coordinating with the boutiques. On my way home, my phone rang. It was Samantha. She sounded distraught. I immediately asked her what was wrong.

"You might want to pull over," she said.

My heart stopped. What was she about to tell me? I pulled over to the side of the road and put my car in park. "What's going on?"

"We have a problem," Samantha said. "I just got a call from the country club. The deposit check of thirty thousand dollars that Karen and Brad wrote didn't clear. If they don't have their money by three p.m. tomorrow, they are canceling the event."

Scrambling for coherency, I sat there in complete shock. I felt like my heart stopped. "Did you reach out to Karen?"

"Yes, several times, and she's not returning my calls."

Oh, God, how could this be? The event was less than forty-eight hours away. There must be a mistake. *Stay calm, stay calm,* I thought. I hung up the phone and immediately started calling Karen. I left multiple messages but didn't hear back. I was panicking. I had upward of $150,000 of merchandise from the most well-known, upscale boutiques in LA. Jewelry stores had already taken out additional insurance, Rolls-Royce had five cars reserved for the ladies, and my own reputation was on the line. It felt like everything was about to fall apart. I stayed up all night pacing and waiting for a return phone call from Karen.

The next morning while running around to finish up the last-minute details, I dialed her number for the tenth time. Her housekeeper finally answered her cell phone. I was panic-stricken. She told me Karen couldn't talk. When I insisted that she get her immediately, she said that Karen was busy handing out flyers at the hotel.

"What!? Handing out flyers for what?" I yelled on the other end.

"For a fashion event tomorrow?" her housekeeper said.

I couldn't believe what she was saying. None of this was making any sense. I demanded that her housekeeper tell her to get the money to the country club in one hour, or tomorrow's event would be canceled.

I sat in my car, my heart beating out of my chest. I was shaking and sweating, all at the same time. It felt like I was in a nightmare, and everything was spiraling out of control. How would I ever show my face again in the fashion world, if this thing unravels now?

Thirty minutes later, I received a text from Karen: "All taken care of, the money is being hand delivered this afternoon. See you tonight at the gala. In love we trust."

My entire body collapsed. *Thank God.* This was such an emotional roller coaster. I finished organizing and packing the car I had rented, with all the perfectly steamed clothes, racks, shoes, jewelry, and bags. I grabbed my new yellow Mary Katrantzou dress and my crystal-embellished satin Christian Louboutin shoes I had splurged on for the gala and headed upstairs to take a shower and get myself ready.

At 4:30 P.M., another text came from Samantha. "Still no money."

I texted Karen, who replied, "Traffic. It's coming." We were down to the wire, and my nerves were shot.

A half hour later, I got a call from the country club's general manager.

"Jen, I'm sorry to inform you, but we are going to cancel the event for tomorrow. I just can't proceed without the deposit money," he said.

"Wait, hold on, Jeff," I pleaded. "They are stuck in traffic. The money is coming. Look, I'm on my way to the gala, and if I have to get the money myself from them and bring it back to you, I will. Give me an hour and a half to sort this out."

"All right, you have an hour and a half. I'll wait to hear from you." In our car on our way to the city, my husband Tony reached over and grabbed my hand and squeezed it tightly and said, "I love you, and I'm proud of you. We will figure this out." It calmed me down. I sat in complete silence the entire drive into the city, praying this would all resolve itself in the way in which it was supposed to. I was mad at myself for ignoring all the signs along the way and equally mad at myself for spending way too much on my outfit to impress these First Ladies.

When we arrived at the Century City Hotel, there was security everywhere. We were stopped and asked to show our identification just to pull into the hotel. Once in front of the hotel, there were men and women of African descent adorned in elaborate and traditional African ceremonial garb. It was beautiful to see and, in some small way, I was relieved that this event wasn't one big hoax. Tony saw Brad in the lobby and turned to me and said, "Stay here."

I sat, watching their interaction from afar and with anticipation. I wanted to get out of the car and start screaming at him but didn't. I could see their conversation was escalating. On the one hand, I didn't want to scuff my new shoes because, if this event wasn't happening, those babies were going back. But I couldn't contain myself any longer. I opened the door and walked straight up to Brad and asked pointedly, "Brad, did you write a check to the country club for thirty thousand dollars knowing you didn't have the funds in your bank account to cover the check?"

"Yes," he said, "but we were promised—"

I interrupted him. "That's a felony, Brad. Where is Karen?"

"She's getting ready."

"Getting ready for what?" I was seething.

"The gala."

I demanded to see her right away, while Brad kept repeating his apology, saying he didn't mean for any of this to happen. Brad proceeded to bring us up to their suite in the hotel, and upon entry, I was in shock. I saw my marketing materials, the same ones that were supposedly delivered to the First Ladies weeks ago, scattered all over the floor in the entry. No wonder

I hadn't received any calls. Next to them were all the gift bags I scrambled to get. I couldn't believe what I saw. *What is happening?* I walked straight into the bathroom, and Karen was sitting on a vanity chair with her back toward me, in the dress and jewelry I had loaned her, applying her makeup.

"Karen!" I yelled. And this was the moment I realized what I was dealing with. She slowly looked over her shoulder, lifted her index finger, and whispered, "Just a minute."

Immediately, I started asking about the money and what the hell was going on. She slowly stood up, turned around, and started screaming back, "Well now you know! There is no money!"

"What do you mean 'there's no money,' Karen? I have everything lined up for tomorrow. Stores have already been delivering merchandise. *Hundreds* of tickets have been sold, cars are scheduled to pick up the First Ladies. What the hell are you talking about?"

That's when she lost it. She started screaming that she had been scammed, that the money never came through, that "they" were all a bunch of liars. I didn't know who "they" were. She was making absolutely no sense. I stared at her in complete disbelief.

She continued ranting about how she was played and that none of this was her fault. Then she said she was going downstairs to the gala to make a public announcement in front of hundreds of guests to clear our names. She would say that Jen Principe did an incredible job and none of this was my fault.

Suddenly Tony interjected.

"Stop," he said. "You will do no such thing. My wife is not involved in this train wreck. Her name is not to be mentioned to anyone ever, or you will have to deal with the consequences of a lawsuit. You will pay my wife the money you owe her, including the money she forwarded you for the picture frames, or we will see you in court." He grabbed my hand and escorted me out of her hotel room.

Once in the elevator, I began bawling hysterically and collapsed in Tony's arms. The elevator doors opened, and we stood there while I cried like a baby. Meanwhile, just outside, all the First Ladies were going about their business—unaware any of this had even occurred. Not one of them was given my styling package or even knew who I was. We sat in the lobby together, deciding what the first next step would be. I called Samantha, and we both cried in disbelief. She agreed to get the list of all the attendees and send out an email informing them that the event was canceled. I then made my way down the list, calling the country club and each vendor and boutique to inform them of the bad news. Those were some of the hardest calls I've ever had to make. I wondered how I could ever show my face again in the fashion industry and if anyone would ever trust me again.

We drove home that night, with my newly scuffed shoes, in silence. I unpacked my car that night and passed out from exhaustion. I was hoping that when I woke up, it would all just be a bad nightmare, but when I looked at all the beautiful clothes sprawled out across my living room that needed to be returned to the boutiques, reality set back in: this was *not* a dream. I was devastated and embarrassed to show my face, but I had to find the strength to move forward. I once again did the only thing I knew how to do. I prayed.

> *Dear God,*
> *I feel weak and defeated.*
> *I want to hide and escape from my fears.*
> *I'm feeling afraid and paralyzed.*
> *Help me to diminish my ego and learn from this experience.*

That next morning, I heard a knock at my front door. It was Samantha and a few of my other closest girlfriends (my favorite sweatshirts). They showed up in the way that best friends do: ready to help me rise from the ashes. I had never been so thankful for my friends and their support, and I honestly don't know if I could have done it without them. We spent that afternoon dismantling the looks with their help, and I found the courage to deliver the clothes back to the boutiques with my head held high. But underneath, I had never been so humiliated in my life.

Samantha found out there were only a handful of tickets sold to the event, and most of them were to our friends and family. I reached out to Carl and found out there was no donation money. He was told by Karen that Tony and I, along with Samantha and Scott, were the donors for the event. Hence, why he was so appreciative at that first meeting. Sadly, I had to take Karen to court to be reimbursed for the frames and the styling fee we agreed upon. Thank goodness I saved every email and every voicemail. I won the case.

In my mind, I thought my reputation had been tarnished, and I decided to shut my business down for close to a year. I was so "in my head" about what everyone would think about me. My ego was shattered, and I felt humiliated. *How will I ever show my face again to all the stores that trusted in me?* I thought.

In my mind, I was a failure and could never redeem myself as a legitimate stylist. This was a dose of humility. But as time passed, I missed my clients and the creativity of styling. But I mostly missed changing people's lives for the better. That's when I remembered one of my favorite quotes by C. S. Lewis (who wrote *The Chronicles of Narnia* and is a devout Christian): "Humility is not thinking less of yourself; it's thinking of yourself less." It was time for me to get back out there and swallow my pride.

I had learned so many valuable business lessons and the consequences of ignoring warning signs. In my own quest for stardom, I put my blinders up, just like Karen did, while trying to force pieces that didn't fit. Hindsight offers us what no one moment in the present is capable of doing and can be our biggest teacher. I often like to play the game of "what if?"

What if Karen came up with the funds at the last minute, and the event happened with only a handful of tickets sold? Or what if Karen's grandiose description of the First Ladies' "retail therapy" spending habits were fabricated? They probably were. All those boutiques would have lost more money and valuable time in the long run. But the biggest question I needed to ask myself was, what if it went off perfectly and my career did take off?

The truth is, I didn't have enough experience, and I wasn't ready. I have had so many lessons along the way that have prepared me for the next chapter in my career. Growing a business takes time, and I was able to use that experience to help me grow at the perfect pace for my family and me. I did pray in the car, on the way to the Gala for the right outcome, and I believe it *was* the right outcome. I will never really know for sure, but I think God protected me from far more damage.

This was a dose of humility. It took time for me to dust myself off and pick myself back up. To my surprise, everyone was glad to see me back in their stores, shopping for my clients again, and had completely forgotten about the event. In just a short time, I was right back to doing what I loved and pulling from all those same stores, like nothing had ever happened. People forget, and life just keeps moving on.

I received a phone call from one of Karen's friends and was told Karen suffers from bipolar disorder. That made perfect sense to me, with all her highs and lows. I have no hard feelings toward Karen. In my heart, I do believe that her intent, in the beginning, was to do good. But her ego got in the way, and she just kept digging a deeper hole and couldn't find a way out. I pray and hope that she, too, has dusted herself off, picked herself back up off the floor, and is living her best life.

I know I am.

CHAPTER 14

The Phoenix Effect

*"It's in the stillness that we detect our soul's inclinations.
The privacy of silence offers us the answers we need."*

—ELEANOR R. BELMONT

When your passion aligns with being of service, I believe you have found your purpose. For me, my passion has always been clothes. But it wasn't until I listened to the whispers of the universe and was called to the fire that I found my purpose.

The phoenix is a legendary radiant mythical firebird, shimmering with luminous shades of gold and scarlet, and is said to live for one thousand years. It was said to have lived in paradise, a land of unimaginable perfection. However, when the bird began to feel the effects of its age, it flew into the mortal world and built a nest of cinnamon and frankincense. It ignites a fire and, just before it dies, surrenders itself to it—bursting into the flames. It is then miraculously reborn, rising out of the fire to start a new, long life.

This story is one of the most well-known ancient myths of the modern day and has a legacy in many cultures and religions. It's a story of rebirth into an even stronger self. And I believe that we are all a part of a "phoenix journey." Sometimes, we help the phoenix reemerge and, other times, we must dive into the fire ourselves. Either way, we are reborn.

I believe that sometimes in order to dive into the fire, you must *listen first for the message* and then have *the courage* to *act* on the God shots. If you remember, my definition of a *God shot* is an intuitive knowing, a gut feeling, a deep intuition, a creative urge that all bear the fingerprints of a divine presence. For some people, the universe whispers the God shots and, for others, it screams to them, loud and clear. For me, it's been a combination of both whispers and screams that have shaped some of the most unique and meaningful experiences of my life.

The most recent example of this happened when I was watching a segment with Dr. Sanjay Gupta on CNN. Kevin Hines was recalling a story about how he survived jumping off the Golden Gate Bridge. Statistically, 98 percent of people don't survive.[12] During the interview, there were two things Kevin said that made the hairs on my arms stand up. First, he had made a pact with himself that if anyone would have been kind to him on that bridge or tried to stop him, he wouldn't have jumped. And second, that the minute his feet left the ground, he had immediate regret. Having lost a very close family member (my sister-in-law) to suicide just five years prior, I've had an intimate understanding of the irreparable damage it can do to those left behind.

When I heard Kevin's words, a current of raw electricity passed through me; maybe my sister-in-law had regret too. I felt my heart compress and I felt sad that entire day. I couldn't get this interview with Kevin out of my head.

Just two days later, my husband and I were invited to a concert. We were running late and still had to pick up another couple along the way. En route, and as Murphy's Law would have it, we got stuck behind every slow driver imaginable. It was almost comical, as if we were being pranked on a hidden-camera show. My husband—who is always on time—started to show his frustration as we proceeded to hit every single red light. He then looked over at me and asked incredulously, "Is this a joke?!"

I laughed and said, "Maybe God's trying to slow us down for something."

We finally arrived at our friends' house ten minutes behind schedule, and the four of us headed off to the concert, hoping there wouldn't be any traffic. I sat in the backseat with my girlfriend, engaging in girl talk, while the boys sat up front and engaged in sports and business. Within a few short minutes, as we were driving toward the overpass, my girlfriend looked up and yelled out, "Holy shit! Is that man going to jump off that bridge?!"

---

12 Wikipedia, s.v. "Suicides at the Golden Gate Bridge," last modified February 26, 2022, https://en.wikipedia.org/wiki/Suicides_at_the_Golden_Gate_Bridge.

We collectively looked up to see a man clinging to the outside of a chain-link fence on the overpass ledge, hanging on for his life. As we continued driving under the bridge, he disappeared from our view. He was gone in an instant. My friend yelled out to call 911, and my husband quickly dialed the emergency line, giving the operator the exact location of the unidentified man, seemingly about to end his life. Suddenly I remembered Kevin Hines.

"Get off the freeway right now. We have to go back!" I yelled out.

Everyone in the car seemed bewildered at my request.

"What? Why?" they said.

"Because Kevin Hines said if someone tried to stop him, he wouldn't have jumped. Quick, get off the freeway *now*!" I screamed, much to their confusion. In support, my girlfriend urged my husband to pull off the freeway too.

As I was explaining Kevin's interview, my husband swerved across four lanes to exit the freeway. We were only one off-ramp away, but I knew time could be running out. We drove as quickly as we could up the frontage road toward the bridge, and when we turned the corner, there he was, hanging on to the fence, cars speeding below him.

We pulled over to the opposite side of the road, and my girlfriend and I ran across the street as fast as we could toward him. The gravity of this situation soon set in. We both realized that if we weren't able to stop him, we would have to emotionally endure witnessing a suicide. We stood on the outside of the fence, our hearts pounding out of our chests, as we came face-to-face with him. I will never forget the look of utter and complete despair in his eyes. *What should I say to him?* I thought. And then the words just fell out of my mouth: "We love you. Please don't jump."

There was a pause, one that felt disproportionately long but was probably mere seconds. I could hear cars coming behind us, the speeding cars below us, sirens approaching, and yet, in this very tense moment, the only thing I could hear was the sound of my heart beating.

"I have nothing to live for. I'm done. I don't want to live anymore," he replied, the hope draining from his face.

My friend placed her hands on the fence, her palms touching his, and began begging him not to take his own life. We kept reminding him that we loved him and that he may feel differently tomorrow.

Then my girlfriend reminded him that he might not only end his life, but that someone innocent below could lose their life too. I could see by the look on his face that this shifted his perspective. His eyes looked down at the speeding cars below him and then back up at us. His eyes softened. My girlfriend put her hands back on the fence, once again her palms on his, and said, "Follow my hands."

We could hear emergency vehicles and police sirens all around us. Four police officers tried to approach us, but the man on the bridge began to panic and yelled out, "No cops, no cops!"

The police officers backed away as they assessed the situation and could see that we seemed to have things under control. My girlfriend once again reminded him to keep his eyes locked onto hers as I kept reassuring him that he is loved.

He began slowly moving his feet, his eyes locked on us. One misstep, and he could plummet to his death on the freeway below. Carefully, one small step at time and with our continued assurance that he was loved, he began making his way off the bridge. Once both of his feet landed safely on the ground, my friend and I collapsed into each other until the adrenaline rush subsided. Once he was safely off the bridge, he was taken by ambulance to the nearest hospital, and we headed off to the concert. Unfortunately, due to HIPAA regulations, I have no idea what happened afterward. I only pray that he found his life worth saving.

That next morning felt surreal. I wondered, what are the chances of hearing Kevin's story and then, just two days later, seeing this man on the bridge ready to take his own life? I reflected on how we got stuck behind every slow driver and hit every red light earlier that evening. Questions flooded my mind: *What if we had been on time or had even passed that bridge just a few minutes earlier? How would his fate have been different? What would have been the outcome for some unknown person or family had he jumped?* I thought about the friend I was with and how, out of all the people I could have been with, she was the most capable to handle this type of situation with me. All the pieces fit perfectly, and I believe, with every fiber in my body, that we were meant to be there.

This is an example of the universe screaming a very loud and clear message. However, some messages are more subtle and require you to tune in more acutely to the universe's inspired utterances. If I quiet my mind and really listen, I can hear them. This is one of the reasons I love to run. Running isn't just my daily dose of meditation, but it's also when I'm filled with inspirational thoughts, direction, and answers. It's within the white space that Juliet Funt so eloquently puts it: "The oxygen that allows everything else to catch fire." It's when I hear the God shots most clearly and gain clarity of my personal life direction, one that takes me out of "self" and into service. I can get into ego, self-pity, and fear too easily, and running is the perfect antidote to those spiritual maladies. Running allows me to connect with my soul's purpose, and I'm able to stay in shape at the same time!

There is a scene in the Queen biopic *Bohemian Rhapsody* when Freddie Mercury, played by Rami Malek, is sitting at the piano and begins to tinker with the opening notes to the now iconic song that shares the movie's title. As he begins to compose, viewers watch as he suddenly receives a burst of inspiration and becomes so overwhelmed with emotion, he has to stop playing and gasps for air.

"Oh, that's good," he says. He knows it and doesn't doubt it. When I saw this, my eyes welled up. I leaned over to my husband and said, "I know that feeling."

I've had it several times even while writing this book. It's as if something is being channeled from outside of you and flows right through you. And when it does, it's an absolute knowing that you must lean into, listen to, and move forward. It was during one of these runs that I was inspired to lean in and start my nonprofit, iStyle Pretty in Pink, which has become one of the most meaningful parts of my styling career and life.

If you're looking at a beautiful mosaic tile ceiling that happens to be missing a tile, what do you concentrate your vision on most? In his book, *Happiness Is a Serious Problem*, Dennis Prager refers to this as the "missing tile syndrome." The one missing thing is the thing we focus on in our lives and can be a huge obstacle to finding true happiness.

For example, perhaps you have acne and you tend to focus on everyone in the room who has perfect skin. For me, it's been the fact that my mom left me when I was six months old and I didn't have a daughter of my own. Of course, I love my sons and I love being a boy mom. But I have always longed for a daughter.

It was during one of my runs when the thought about *not* being a girl mom started to sink in. Throughout motherhood, I have heard over and over again about how boys leave their moms when they get married, but girls never do. I started going down a rabbit hole of self-pity and began focusing on the missing tile when a voice in my head said, "*Stop.*" I, figuratively and literally, came to a screeching halt. Then the next thing I heard was a voice whisper, "Give your gift away."

The words kept ringing in my head. "Give your gift away. Give your gift away."

And then it struck me, and the floodgates opened: *What if I could use my styling skills to personalize and curate transformational photoshoot experiences for girls with cancer?* If you have never had a photoshoot before, I highly recommend it. It's so much fun and, as a stylist, I get to create the overall vision beyond just the clothing, hair, and makeup. And almost every little girl I've met loves to play dress-up.

My idea was that the experience I would provide would be more than just a photoshoot; I would be creating a chance for them to escape from their illness and feel like a prince/princess, an athlete, or a celebrity for the day. Whatever it is that they dream about, I would help create through their wardrobe. At the end of each shoot, the families would receive a custom coffee table photo book of their child to keep. As these ideas continued to flow in and through me, the floodgates opened and I, too, gasped for air, as the tears ran down my face. Like Freddie Mercury in that moment of inspiration from *Bohemian Rhapsody*, I knew it was right, and I also knew I needed to take action right away.

I suddenly remembered a beautiful young woman in my neighborhood whom I adored because of her huge heart. She was an extremely talented singer and used to spend some of her spare time in a children's hospital singing to a young girl during her cancer treatments. I called Gaby from the side of the road that morning and told her my idea; she loved it immediately, saying it brought her to tears. Gaby gave me the young girl's father's phone

number, and what happened next was nothing short of the universe conspiring and the divine pushing things in motion. I dialed the phone number she
gave me and heard a man's voice pick up.

"Is this Jeff?" I asked.

"Yes, how can I help you?" the voice on the other end replied.

"Hello, Jeff. My name is Jen, and I got your number from Gaby. I'm a
friend of hers and I understand you have a daughter named Zoe who has
been in treatment for cancer."

"Um, yes, I do. What can I do for you?"

"Well, I am a wardrobe stylist, and I wanted to offer Zoe a day to feel like
a princess and give her a customized photoshoot. There's no cost involved,
Jeff. It's just my way of giving back," I said.

There was a long pause.

"Wait. Is this Jen Principe?" he asked.

"Yes, it is," I said, surprised.

"Jen, this is Jeff Feldman. I was Jeremy's first baseball coach!"

Turns out, Jeff and my husband coached my son's first baseball team
together. It had been at least six years since we last spoke. I didn't realize he
had another child. I couldn't believe it. *What were the chances?* Yet I *could*
believe it. There's a Hebrew word known as *b'sheret*, which means "meant to
be, inevitable, or preordained." I knew it was *b'sheret*.

At six years old, Zoe became my first model. We had a tea party, baked
cupcakes, and played my version of dress-up, which meant she was styled
head to toe with each activity that we did. Every picture was more beautiful
than the next, as Zoe radiated her light and embraced every moment. When
I gave the book to her parents, they were in tears as each page captured the
essence of her lively spirit. Seeing their daughter just being a little girl and
feeling healthy brought so much joy into their lives. Being a part of that
experience was like a drug for me; I was hooked.

I continued to be referred to by other children and then, one day,
I received a phone call from a high school student named Shendell, a teenager with cerebral palsy, who was interested in having her own *Pretty in Pink*
session. Shendell's was one of my favorite photoshoots because she wouldn't
allow her visible disability to get in the way of her life and has used her

photos to inspire others. She is still a part of my life and, incidentally, calls me her second mom. I guess daughters can manifest in many ways.

Sadly, I lost daughters too. It's one of the most challenging aspects of being assigned this role. At the beginning of COVID-19, Cammy's (whom I photographed three years prior) melanoma returned suddenly, and aggressively, and she lost her battle at the young age of twenty. At her funeral, I met her best friend Sienna, who also had cancer. Several weeks later, I offered her a photoshoot to help lift her spirits. In the interim, I kept in touch with Cammy's mother and learned that one of Cammy's favorite things to do was to go to Disneyland; she had an unfulfilled wish of sending all the girls in her cancer support group to the happiest place on earth. When she told me this, the wheels started turning; I had another God shot.

I called Sienna, Cammy's best friend, and suggested that we do a modern-day Disney shoot in honor of Cammy. It was serendipitous because I had been telling my husband for the last five years that, one day, I wanted to do a Cinderella photoshoot, complete with the glass slippers, blue gown, and old-fashioned carriage. And that's exactly what I did. But the real miracle was the day I delivered Sienna her book to her home shortly after the photoshoot. When I arrived, she asked if she could show me something. She escorted me up the stairs to her bedroom and slowly opened the door. What I saw before me literally took my breath away. Above her bed was a colorful mural she'd had since she was a little girl: Cinderella in her blue gown and glass slippers. I knew that God had a hand in this one too. The day of the photoshoot was one of the most magical days of my life.

I continued shooting girls for several years when a woman reached out to me through Instagram. Becky, a former model who lived in Salt Lake City, suffered from muscular dystrophy and had gotten into a horrible accident in her wheelchair. She has had upward of seventy surgeries and is unable to lift her arms above her chest. Becky was hoping I could help find a solution to help her dress more easily. She wore shirts in size extra-large so that they'd be easier for her to maneuver over her head, but they hung loosely off her small shoulders.

After some research, my husband was able to help her find an apparatus that could assist her in dressing, and I suggested we also make some custom clothes with Velcro closures. We became fast friends on social media. Becky would periodically send me updates of her life along with her service dog, Ella. She expressed to me that she dreamed of one day modeling again. She was also planning a trip to California to meet with a few medical specialists. Naturally, I offered her a *Pretty in Pink* experience during her visit; Becky was elated and couldn't wait for the experience.

Several weeks later, though, I received a letter from Becky with some dreadful news. Her lungs were no longer emitting carbon dioxide. Her condition was terminal. I could feel the despair and sheer terror in her messages. I couldn't stop thinking about her and could feel her light diminishing. I decided to fly my team to Salt Lake City to make one of her bucket list wishes come true. Becky was going to model again, and we were going to bring out her inner goddess.

Meeting Becky for the first time was surreal. I felt like I had already known her, like our souls had been connected before. Although in a wheelchair, complete with an oxygen tank to breathe, Becky was fully alive and her spirit was delightfully childlike. She beamed with excitement and enthusiasm that was contagious, engulfing us all. The looks I chose for her were ethereal and feminine, representing her true nature. She once told me she felt as if she were trapped in her own body, so in one of her looks, I used a butterfly halo that cascaded around her head and through her hair. We watched her on-camera transformation as she went from a caterpillar to a beautiful butterfly, a complete metamorphosis before our eyes. The day flew by and, sadly, we had to say goodbye to Becky and Ella. That's always the hardest part about my nonprofit: saying goodbye. This is the letter I received from Becky afterward:

> *I met Jen through Instagram. I saw her talent for clothes and style. I reached out to her and shared my story. I was born with spina bifida and was later diagnosed with muscular dystrophy. My muscles deteriorated so much so that it's become almost impossible to dress myself anymore. Sometimes I end up wearing the same clothes for a week because I just don't have the strength to change.*

I was in a terrible wheelchair accident and have had 72 surgeries since, one that required me to stay in bed for a full year to heal. If I thought I knew pain before, it was nothing compared to now. The aftereffect of being in a body cast for that long has taken a toll on my health. I even had trouble breathing. Recently, I was diagnosed with hypercapnia, and my lungs have begun to collapse. I was recently told my condition has become terminal.

Jen knew I had modeled in the past. She knew my style and my hopes to model at least one more time again before I can't anymore. She knew how I felt about my diagnosis, my looks, my fears, my hopes. I didn't really have to tell her much. She is so intune, she just knew.

She also knew I was too sick to travel to California, and when she told me she was coming to see me, I felt my heart beat so hard for the first time since my diagnosis. I started to feel a little more hope, a little more alive; she gave me something to look forward to.

When I met Jen and her team, my heart was full and tears ran down my face from the joy I felt. Everyone on her team was professional, kind, and fun. The moment I rolled my wheelchair through the door, it felt so magical, as if I were in a dream. Suddenly I was back to my modeling days. My body was feeling the same strength as my spirit. For a few hours, I could turn back time and not feel sick.

Each outfit Jen picked for me had a special meaning. There is one where I'm wearing this beautiful scarf, as if I'm going to sail away and everything is all right; another where she put butterflies in my hair. It felt symbolic, for my body felt like it was trapped in a cocoon, and with the help of her team, I felt as free as a butterfly! I was wearing makeup, which I hadn't done since my terminal diagnosis. I felt beautiful, classy, sassy, and bold. I had no fear and had longed to feel that way one more time.

The icing on the cake was her dressing my service dog, Ella, who developed a crush on Jen's sweet husband, Tony. This treasured gift doesn't just remain in my mind or my heart. It has changed me! It has given me strength to move forward and accept what life throws at me. I can look at these pictures and feel my power and the fullness of my heart. I can treasure the memory of the laughter and love that I experienced that day. I truly felt like a phoenix rising from the ashes! My cup runneth over.

The day I received this letter, I went on a run and started thinking about the legend of the phoenix once again and how we are all "called to the fire." Sometimes, we are just a part of the process in helping the phoenix rise from the ashes, as was my role with Becky and many others. But other times we *are* the phoenix. Perhaps we are called to the fire by way of illness or trauma, requiring us to dive into the flames to reignite parts of ourselves that have become dormant or lost. Maybe that's leaving a marriage, a job, or a friendship—something where we must find the courage to take the risk and fly into the flames to birth a newer version of ourselves, a version that has been waiting to be born. Or maybe it has to do with addiction or mental health, choosing not to jump off the bridge and choosing life instead. Or perhaps it's as simple as listening to the sound of silence, hearing your calling, and acting on it.

As I was running, I began to reflect on the inception of *Pretty in Pink* and all the little girls who have since come into my life. I realized I had lots of daughters, after all. I thought about my three nephews and how they lost their mom and how much they needed my presence in their lives too. My personal mosaic was beautiful. It may appear to be missing a tile, but if I take a step back and look at it in its totality, it's just a matter of perception. It isn't missing a tile at all; it never really was. I started thinking that *Pretty in Pink* needed to evolve once again to include all genders.

But what will I call it?

I closed my eyes, turning toward the warmth of the sunlight, and spread my arms as far as I could expand them, like a bird taking flight. I could feel the cool breeze on my face and the wind blowing through my hair as each foot hit the pavement. I drew in a long, deep breath. I could feel it coming. I was connecting to the source within me. And then, there it was. I stopped, and once again, I gasped for air and my eyes welled up. Sometimes, the answers are *so* obvious, but for whatever reason—our own myopia, perhaps—we just can't see them. It had been there all along. I opened my eyes, looked up, and thanked the universe once again for weaving another thread into my life story. That's how the "Phoenix Effect" was born.

To learn more about the Phoenix Effect, visit http://jpstyles.com/giving-back.

Style isn't just about one thing. Just like styling a photoshoot, it's about the details and creating an entire vision for yourself every time you get dressed. Your hair, makeup, and accessories can elevate, enhance, and complete the perfect look. Grab your phone and hit the QR code now to learn the dos and don'ts of how to accessorize like a pro.

VIDEO TUTORIALS

CHAPTER 15

It's in the Blood

"We are never divorced from our past, that is where our roots lie. We can gain strength and comfort knowing that our past experiences are not coincident."

—UNKNOWN

There are two things that have always been at the core of my being: faith and fashion. Both have served huge parts in supporting me through some of the most painful and challenging times in my life; they've also oriented my growth, teaching me some of the most valuable lessons I needed to learn. Faith has carried me through my darker moments, when my light was dim, when I stopped believing in myself. It has propelled me forward and given me the courage I have needed to take risks when the universe whispered to me and my soul called out. Faith has given me the strength to continue to move forward when I didn't think I could. I believe without it, I would be in a very different place in my life today. My steadfast belief in something bigger than myself has granted me the bravery to look inward and battle my shadow self and my character defects without punishing myself. We all have them. It has taught me about acceptance and forgiveness and, most importantly, has shown me that one way to healing is through service.

Fashion, clothes specifically, brought an enormous amount of joy not only to my own life but also to that of my clients. Being a stylist has been a healthy outlet for me and allowed my creativity to flow. Clothes have enhanced some of my most memorable experiences and also enabled me to recapture and hold on to the memories of past loved ones. They have served as a healing modality. But more than that, fashion has shown me there is space in the spiritual realm for the material too.

Through my fashion journey, I've been able to use my gift to help others feel more confident and help my clients and friends begin transforming from the outside *in*.

Wardrobe and fashion have helped those who have felt they have lost parts of their identity reignite them anew, birthing evolved versions of themselves via the joy clothes bring into their lives. But the most unique part of my own personal journey is how those two things have been so tightly intertwined throughout my life. If we really take the time to look a little closer at our day-to-day experiences in life, I believe we can find the lessons and the hidden deeper meanings that can transform, if we let it. Sometimes, they reveal themselves when we least expect it. It's just a matter of the lenses we choose to use to look at things.

I have always wondered why these two things—faith and fashion—have played such an integral part in my life. I remember as a child being told that God was *everywhere*. I took this literally, and one day my father came into my room and found me kissing the walls, the carpet, the chair, and the mirror. Perplexed, he asked me what I was doing. I told him I was "kissing God."

Today, I don't go around kissing objects, but I still believe that God really *is* everywhere and speaks to and *through* us. In fact, I believe God has been speaking to me since I was a child, in the one language I understood: clothing. We all have a gift to share; it can be as subtle as being a great listener, to being athletic, like being a phenomenal basketball player and using your platform to inspire others, like Kobe Bryant did. Sometimes, I wonder if being the granddaughter of a tenth-generation rabbi has imbued me with a strong belief in a higher power because it's in my blood.

Initially, I wasn't going to write about my mother and our relationship because it's a sensitive subject for both of us and quite complicated. As I sat in my bed debating with myself about whether I should open up this can of worms, I suddenly remembered once again that clothes were the common thread that brought the two of us together and would, again, teach me some of the most valuable lessons I have ever learned about acceptance and forgiveness. This is one story that needs to be told.

My mother tried to have a relationship with me throughout my childhood; however, I had formed a strong bond with Tia since she was my sole caretaker from infancy. On the weekends, I spent most of my time with my Bubbie and my aunt. When my mother *did* come around, which wasn't often, I rejected her and, over time, the less effort she put in. There is nothing conventional about her. She's quirky, eccentric, flamboyant at times, free-spirited—a wild gypsy soul and an artist. She's certainly not the mother I fantasized about having when I was little. I envisioned the iconic Mrs. Brady from *The Brady Bunch* or Clair Huxtable from *The Cosby Show*. In a nutshell, I wished my mother came in a better package. I wanted the perfectly domesticated TV-ready mother who sewed, baked pies, packed lunches, and drove carpool. I wanted a mother who was sophisticated, beautiful, wise, and, of course, dressed like a movie star.

My biological mother and I are opposites. If you saw us together in a room, I guarantee you'd never believe we are related. My mother mostly looked like she didn't care about her appearance, which made me uncomfortable as hell. My mom once told me that she wanted to meet someone and she was lonely. When I suggested that she put a little more effort into her appearance, she said, "I just want to be loved as I am. I don't want to waste my time."

My memories of my mother growing up are far and few between because she wasn't around much. When I had black eyes and bloody noses from the wrath of Tia's outbursts, my mother was nowhere to be found. But when it was time to celebrate Mother's Day, a birthday, or a graduation, she seemed to always show up and take pride in her three children. I hated that. The "story" I replayed in my head and shared with others was that I was abandoned. I used that as an excuse for attention and self-pity. I also blamed my mom for subjecting me to Tia's abuse and, over time, most, if not all, of my character defects. I had such anger and resentment toward her that I put my armor up all around me every time she tried to have a relationship with me. But to her credit, in her way, she never stopped trying.

One day, when I was nineteen years old, my mom got a job as a bookkeeper for a men's shirt line called Eton of Sweden. She reached out to me, raving about the shirts, claiming they were timeless and fashionable and made of the best quality fabrics. Honestly, I knew nothing about men's shirts and wasn't all that interested until she said that they needed a female model for an upcoming campaign and thought I would be perfect for it. She also wanted me to meet her new friend Kurt who was the rep for the company and would be responsible for bringing the shirt line to the US. I agreed to meet Kurt and see the shirts, mainly because I was interested in the modeling gig. To my surprise, my mom was right. The shirts were great, and I immediately fell in love with Kurt and his boyfriend.

Kurt and I became fast friends, but I soon found myself in a precarious situation because he was also very good friends with my mom. He adored my mom and kept pushing and encouraging me to let her into my life. I found myself inadvertently spending time with my mother because of Kurt. I would show up at one of his parties and, lo and behold, there she was, a joint in one hand and a cigarette in the other. She never hid who she was from me or from anyone. Being in a social setting where I wasn't forced to have a relationship with her made it easier for me to slowly let go of my armor. I stopped seeing her as the mother who had left me and started seeing her as just another person, who happened to be at the same party I was. And I began seeing parts of her personality that I really liked. My mom is a "what you see is what you get" kind of woman; she has no filter, she's fun, silly, intelligent, and she knows how to have a good time. But the one thing that stood out to me that I admire most about her was how nonjudgmental she is. And those things that I thought were quirky and weird were now somewhat refreshing to me.

A few months later, Kurt asked me to go to Las Vegas for the apparel trade show "Magic" on behalf of Eton since I had modeled for the line. Technically, I would be considered an employee, and it would be an all-expenses-paid trip, which, at the time, sounded amazing since I couldn't afford a trip to Vegas on my own. The only caveat was that I would be rooming with my mom. This made me a little nervous, as it would be the first time she and I would be away together and sleeping in the same room that I could remember.

As the evening fell that first night in Vegas, and as we were getting ready for bed, my mother pulled something out from the hotel dresser drawer. She held a brown paper bag in her hand and came toward me slowly, sitting on the corner of my bed. With the bag close to her chest, she cleared her throat. I could see she was nervous, and so was I. I had no idea what she was about to say or do, but my mom had a knack for giving unusual gifts.

Her voice cracked for a moment before she said, "Jenny, I'm really glad we are spending this time together. I have something for you. But before I give it to you, I want you to know something."

I stiffened.

"What I want you to know is that I love you, and I have loved you since the day you were born. I want more than anything to have a relationship with you," she said. She paused and started getting teary-eyed. I began to feel uncomfortable. Her sincerity aside, I honestly had just hoped we could have a weekend away together without her trying to force our relationship.

She wiped tears from her eyes, gathered her composure, and continued. "I bought this for you a long time ago when I was in Paris and have been waiting for the right time to give it to you."

She pulled out a small Parisian porcelain doll and handed it to me. It was delicate and actually quite beautiful. It felt strange to be nineteen years old and getting a doll from your mother as a gift, but something about the gesture felt sweet and innocent.

I held the doll in my hand and admired the details of her tiny clothing. She wore a red plaid overall dress with a red, knit long-sleeve turtleneck that had delicate lace around the edge of the sleeves and a matching plaid corduroy cap.

"I named her Amy because *Amie* is the French word for *friend*," my mother said. Then she held my hand and looked me in the eyes. "So, do you think that we could just start by being friends?"

At that moment, I saw my mom in a different light. As she stood there, I could feel her years of pain, brokenness, and vulnerability. She looked like a fragile, wounded child to me and, for the first time ever, I felt sorry for her.

That night, I began to take some of my well-worn armor off and decided to slowly let her into my life. We made some progress, but it was no bed of roses and was painful for the both of us. I was still filled with resentments.

When I was pregnant with my first child, a lot of those old feelings, which up until then had been buried deeply within me, came bubbling up.

I still couldn't understand how she could have "abandoned" me. I would have killed for my unborn child already and couldn't fathom ever leaving him.

One night, I woke up to the cries of my new baby boy. Half-asleep and exhausted, I went into his room and picked him up out of his crib. I sat in the rocking chair and pressed his tiny body against my chest. I inhaled the sweet, intoxicating smell of his skin. I could see the moon seeping through the wooden blinds, and it felt like all time had stopped. I took it all in because I knew that, while it *felt* like time stood still, it was indeed moving too fast and those precious moments would become memories far too soon. He was already six months old, exactly the same age I was when my mom left. As I held my newborn son and rocked him as he nursed, I stared into his innocent, big brown eyes. I suddenly understood that my mother wasn't healthy, because it is impossible for a mother to leave her child unless she is emotionally or spiritually ill.

Another layer of resentment lifted that night with this new realization: I asked my mom to tell me her side of the story of why she left our family, and I resolved to listen with an open heart. And I was right: my mom wasn't well. She struggled with substance abuse and the ramifications of my father's infidelity; in her words, he "couldn't keep his penis in his pants." I also found out that they were separated when I was conceived and that she never intended to have another child and just leave. It was a sad story, to be sure, and it shed some light on why she left, but it wasn't quite enough; I was still resentful and guarded.

One afternoon, several years ago, before I did my mental file cabinet cleaning on my spiritual cleanse retreat, while on a walk with a new friend, we started sharing our pasts to get to know each other. She asked about my upbringing, so I naturally started from the beginning. She listened about how my mother abandoned me when I was six months old, the same story I had been repeating to myself and to anyone who asked. My friend was kind and caring as she listened. When I was finished, she looked at me and said, "So, is that the truth, or is that *your* story?"

"Wait, what did you just ask me?" I replied, taken aback by her question.

"Is that the truth, or is that your story?"

"What? What does that mean?" I asked. I could feel myself getting defensive.

In a very nonjudgmental way, she told me that sometimes our "stories" become our truth because we replay them over and over again until we believe them to be absolute.

To be completely honest, I didn't like what she was saying. I thought, *I want to get done with this walk as soon as possible and erase this conversation from my mind.*

But weeks after our walk together, I couldn't stop thinking about her question.

"Is that the truth, or is that *your* story?"

It felt heavy, frightening; like she handed me an enormous key to Pandora's box. And yet, I felt compelled to use the key.

"To find the truth, ask yourself where you are being selfish and dishonest," she said.

I began to question everything.

So, I set out on a quest to find my truth, which was not an easy task because I had to set my ego aside. I started with asking myself, *How am I being dishonest?* I meditated on this thought for a long time. Then one day, while on a run, the truth came to me. My mother didn't abandon me. The truth is, my mother and father got a divorce when I was six months old, but I was never abandoned. Just realizing that and saying it out loud felt so honest and liberating. I reflected back to the night when I was holding my son and the epiphany I had: that my mother wasn't well. I stopped for a moment, closed my eyes, and imagined what it would have been like living in her shoes. My heart softened, and then I realized how I was being selfish: I had only been looking at our situation from *my* perspective, from *my* wound. It must have been equally painful for my mother to leave her three children. Ultimately, she did what she thought was best for us by giving my father custody.

I also imagined how difficult it must have been when I preferred Flora's company over hers whenever she would come visit me. And most importantly, I realized I didn't accept her for who she was because she wasn't living up to my standard of what I wanted and my expectations.

I remembered one of my favorite quotes: "Sometimes, God gives us what we need, not what we want." I am far more resilient, and my life has led me on this amazing journey because of my mother, not despite her. She might not be the mother I dreamed of or had hoped for, but she is *my* mother and was given to me for a reason.

I also realized that Tia was sick too and in the grip of a terrible disease. There is no excuse for child abuse. However, she also nurtured me as an infant, took care of all my basic needs, and loved me deeply when I was a very young child. It took a long time for me to see the light and get into a place of gratitude. We can hold two conflicting and complex truths. She was a monster, yet I'm grateful.

I also understood that she lived with rampant infidelity and likely felt trapped because my father was also raising her son, whom I've always considered my blood brother. I learned to forgive for the apology I was never going to receive from Tia and let those resentments go too. It was time for me to also forgive my mother. There is a word in Hebrew called *achzarit*, which translates to "the cruel one." It is cruel to be unforgiving if someone has truly repented and sought your forgiveness, which my mother has done plenty of times. I was being punishing and cruel, and it was time to put the past behind me and truly forgive her. In doing so, I realized that I no longer wanted or needed to tell that "story." That felt so freeing.

Sadly, Kurt passed away from AIDS. I miss him and think about him often, especially when I'm out shopping at Neiman Marcus or Saks Fifth Avenue picking up an Eton shirt for one of my male clients. Funny enough, it's one of the more popular shirts I still sell to men, nearly thirty years later.

I also think about that friend I went walking with that day and how her courage to call me out helped change my perspective on one of the biggest parts of my life story. Our friendship was short-lived because she moved away just several weeks later, and we lost touch. But I am thankful she pushed me to let go of the big lie, the monster lurking in the woods. It's interesting to think about the people who come in and out of our lives and the lessons they can teach us if we let them. Sometimes, it's not the ones we are closest to, but the unexpected strangers who can lead us in a completely different direction if we're open to it. Like the story of Henry and how one little act of kindness—by my son Drew—taught us about the importance of giving and receiving; had Henry not been willing to accept Drew's proposal, we all wouldn't have benefitted from that life-changing experience. I think about Bianca and how she taught me, through dance, about confidence and loving the skin you're in; how Maura taught me about the importance of cleaning out the mental clutter in my mind that was holding me back from my potential, propelling me back to my authentic self; how Jill and I may appear to be vastly different on the outside but how similar our humanity is on the inside.

We all share the same struggles; how Zhi taught me about letting go of expectations and how her role wasn't to fill a void I had, but rather a truth to be accepted; my short encounter with Shenzu taught me about attachments and letting go of outcomes; and how the Phoenix Effect has taught me that we are all called to the fire at some point in our lives and the importance of helping someone else rise from the ashes. There are life lessons all around us; we just need to be willing to get a pair of (stylish) glasses so we can see them. Pain pushes us, and I'm grateful that all these strangers forced me to look inward and probe the depths to examine the cracks.

Today my mother and I have a friendship. She makes no excuses for who she is, admits she's made a lot of mistakes, and has punished herself for a long time because of them. I appreciate her honesty, but most of all, I appreciate how accepting she is of herself and of others. As I was debating that night whether to write this chapter, I had an urge to ask my mother about my ancestors. I had never really been curious before. I called my mom and asked her about my grandfather and my great-grandfather because I knew nothing about them. I surprised her with a phone call one day, asking what her father and my grandfather did for a living.

"Oh, I never told you?" she said. "Well, your great-grandfather worked in women's fashion for a company in New York City called Kaplan and Elias. And your grandfather always loved fashion too, and he owned his own manufacturing company in Massachusetts that designed and manufactured dresses for little girls and their matching dolls called Copy-Cat."

I couldn't believe it. I got chills all over my body.

"What? Both my great-grandfather and grandfather were in fashion? Why didn't you tell me this before?" I asked, incredulous.

"I did tell you," she said. "I don't think you were all that interested."

Maybe I not only needed a new set of glasses but also a new set of hearing aids. That night lying there in my bed, I thought about the doll my mother gifted me and how both my grandfather and great-grandfather worked in fashion. I never did get to meet either of them because they passed away before I was born, and my Zayde, the rabbi (my father's father), passed away when I was two. But I'm quite certain I would have loved them both. Thinking about them and their backgrounds, I couldn't help but feel that they have been here all along, guiding me and helping the universe sew the threads into the unique pattern of my life story. I suddenly understood why faith and fashion have been such a huge part of my life.

It's literally in my blood.

AFTERWORD

I often think back to the comment that the BBC producer made about my being born in a Fabergé egg and how my appearance and lifestyle impacted the lens through which she judged me. At first, it made me laugh, but just like my father's advice about my friends being like clothes in my closet, there's some profound wisdom in her analogy.

The way I see it, I *was* like a Fabergé egg for decades. I was protecting my fragile shell with my defense mechanisms and my ego and adorning it with fashionable clothes to hide the cracks. I was afraid that if I let people see my egg in its raw form, with all its imperfections, they might cause another fracture in my shell. I don't think I'm unique in my fears and, quite frankly, I think there are a lot of Fabergé eggs walking this earth, afraid to reveal themselves and judging our personified exteriors. While my job is to help you dress up your "egg" so that you feel confident and empowered, I've learned that sometimes the ones with the most cracks wear the most amount of armor.

Today, I'm thankful for my upbringing—for all its challenges and difficult life lessons. Each story was another chip in my shell. I didn't realize that the fractures were necessary for *me* to be "cracked" wide open. What I feared the most freed me. This need—to be free and born or reborn, to be liberated from whatever closes us off and keeps us small—is *a common thread* I believe we have in all our lives.

Hiring your own personal stylist is a luxury that most people simply can't afford. It's been a dream of mine to provide a styling platform that is affordable while continuing to raise funds for The Phoenix Effect. You can help make my dream a reality by joining the membership and recommending this book to your friends and family.

By joining the membership, filled with educational tutorials, now you, too, can have your own personal stylist without the hefty price tag. Together, we will find your unique style to empower you to step out into the world and feel more confident and fashionable.

Thank you for helping me make my dreams a reality and purchasing *A Common Thread*.

Ten percent of all net proceeds go directly to The Phoenix Effect.

ACKNOWLEDGMENTS

To God, for empowering me to write this book and allowing me to be your vessel.

To my husband, Tony, my soul mate. For your consistency, courage, and strength. For loving all sides of me, supporting my dreams, and seeing my potential when I couldn't.

To my sons, Jeremy and Drew, who healed me through your love.

To my Aunt Feigie, for making me feel seen, heard, and loving me like I was your own daughter.

To my Bubbie, for giving me a safe place to escape to on the weekends.

To Dolly, for your unconditional love and being my biggest cheerleader.

To Quetta, for nurturing my entire family and being the best role model for a mother.

To Rebecca, my soul sister, my rock. For nurturing my soul and loving me unconditionally. I don't know who I would be without you.

To Jen, my *first* best friend in this life. Who witnessed it all, who comforted my wounds and reminded me of my strength, who encouraged me to be like Nemo and just keep swimming.

To Jen Cooper, for your loyalty and always remembering to call me on December 24, the day my father left this earth.

To all my favorite wardrobe friends—and you know who you are—for your support.

To Mordecai Finely, for nurturing my family's souls.

To my mother, for choosing to give me life.

I couldn't have done this without *each and every* one of you.

ABOUT THE AUTHOR

Jen Principe

Jen Principe is a personal and celebrity stylist whose empowering work in fashion has been featured on Hallmark's *Home & Family*, the *Associated Press*, and *Inside Edition*. In 2021, she was featured as a top celebrity LA stylist on *Inside Beverly Hills* (BBC Network). She hosts the KTLA segment "How to Be Your Own Personal Stylist" and has styled for *Focus, JMG, Calabasas Style, Ventura Blvd*, and *Sherwood Life* magazines. Jen is the founder and owner of the nonprofit Phoenix Effect, where she raises funds and curates photoshoots for people suffering from life-debilitating diseases and trauma. She lives in Southern California with her husband and two boys and is the author of *A Common Thread: A Fashion for the Soul Book*.

Connect with the Author

Website: jpstyles.com
Email: jen@jpstyles.com
Instagram: instagram.com/jenprincipestyles
TikTok: tiktok.com/@jenpstyles
LinkedIn: linkedin.com/in/jennifer-principe-901291191

Leave a Review

If you enjoyed *A Common Thread*, please leave a review on the platform of your choice. Reviews help self-published authors find readers like you.